BLUE WALL OF SILENCE: PERCEPTIONS OF THE INFLUENCE OF TRAINING

ON LAW ENFORCEMENT SUICIDE

by

Olivia N. Johnson

A Dissertation Presented in Partial Fulfillment

of the Requirements for the Degree

Doctor of Management in Organizational Leadership

UNIVERSITY OF PHOENIX

February 2010

BLUE WALL OF SILENCE: PERCEPTIONS OF THE INFLUENCE OF TRAINING

ON LAW ENFORCEMENT SUICIDE

by

Olivia N. Johnson

February 2010

Approved:

Karen Bammel, Ph.D., Mentor

Macharia Waruingi, M.D., D.H.A., Committee Member

Orlando Ramos, Ph.D., Committee Member

Accepted and Signed: _Karen Bammel_____ 2/16/2010
Karen Bammel   Date

Accepted and Signed: _Macharia Waruingi____ 2/16/2010
Macharia Waruingi   Date

Accepted and Signed: _Orlando Ramos_____ 3/16/2010
Orlando Ramos   Date

_____ 3/8/2010
Jeremy Moreland Ph.D.   Date
Dean, School of Advanced Studies
University of Phoenix

DEDICATION

Michael J. Miller (04/16/80 - 08/24/06)

Good-bye, brother in blue all of us are thinking of you.

You left this world way too soon, for reasons only known to you.

If only one of us knew, we certainly would have reached out to you.

Good-bye, brother in blue. Rest in peace, Police 31,

Police 31, 10-42

RIP J.D.

ACKNOWLEDGMENTS

I would first like to thank God for making this journey possible. Next, I would like to thank my family for their support and understanding. Lastly, to my friends and peers whose encouragement has inspired me to reach my goals.

I would like to thank the numerous individuals and organizations who have dedicated their lives to saving lives, to the thousands of officers who took their lives before help arrived, to the officers, friends, and families left behind the devastation, and to the men and women in blue who may need mental health assistance in the future.

I would also like thank Rev. Robert Douglas, Director of the National P.O.L.I.C.E. Suicide Foundation and his colleagues for their enlightenment of the topic of police suicide. To New Jersey State Trooper, Dr. Orlando Ramos also of the National P.O.L.I.C.E. Suicide Foundation for his dedication to my cause and the sheer determination to train and educate law enforcement personnel on the topic of police suicide.

I would like to thank my mentor Dr. Karen Bammel for her perseverance and courage presented through the dissertation process. Dr. Bammel, thank you for everything. In addition, I would like to thank committee member Dr. Macharia Waruingi for his personal and professional support towards my cause. Dr. Waruingi you are a true blessing and words cannot express how much you contributed to my success. Dr. Ramos your dedication to recognizing and educating officers on the topic of police suicide has greatly influenced my path. Lastly, and most importantly, to the officers who agreed to participate in the study, may God Bless every one of you. Your participation will assist in saving the lives of your brothers and sisters in blue.

TABLE OF CONTENTS

LIST OF TABLES

Chapter 1: Introduction

Suicide is a public health concern of epidemic proportions (Center for Disease Control [CDC], 2005; Satcher, 1999). Approximately 1 million people commit suicide worldwide every year, which are more individuals than those killed by war and homicide (World Health Organization [WHO], 2006, p. 2). Suicide is the ninth leading cause of death among all age groups and the fourth leading cause of death for individuals between the ages of 18 and 65 in the United States (Andrew, 2008; CDC, 2005; National Center for Health Statistics [NCHS], 2005; Satcher, 1999). Approximately 80 completed suicides occur daily in the United States, with daily suicide attempts as high as 1,500 (NCHS, 2005, p. 1). Heightened risk of suicide exists within intricate subcultures, such as law enforcement, due to the increased levels of stress and trauma. Law enforcement officers are killing themselves at a higher rate than die in the line-of-duty (Kelly & Martin, 2006; Violanti, 2007). According to Tate (2004), law enforcement officers are killing themselves at a rate of seven times that of the general population (para. 1).

The focus in chapter 1 is a discussion on information concerning contributing factors for suicide and why law enforcement officers are at high-risk for suicide. Further, chapter 1 contains a description of the methodology, research design, and the significance to leadership. Chapter 1 concludes with information deemed important to leadership about the implications of law enforcement suicide and possible implications of mental health training on the incidence of law enforcement suicide.

Background of the Problem

Individuals who work in occupations with increased levels of stress, trauma, and identifiable social roles are frequently susceptible to suicide (Cross & Ashley, 2004;

Waters & Ussery, 2007). One occupational category where individuals are exposed to increased levels of stress and trauma, with identifiable social roles, is law enforcement (Violanti et al., 2007; Waters & Ussery, 2007). Long-term effects of stress include the inability of law enforcement officers to cope effectively with daily situations (Waters & Ussery, 2007). White, males between 35 and 54 years of age account for the second highest number of suicides in the United States, second only to elderly White males between the ages of 65 and 85 (CDC, 2005; NCHS, 2005).

From 2004 to 2008, an average of 163 law enforcement officers died in the line-of-duty each year (Officer Down Memorial Page [ODMP], 2004, 2005, 2006, 2007, 2008). During the same 5-year period, law enforcement suicides averaged 429 per year, contributing to a 500% increase in law enforcement deaths nationwide (O'Hara, 2009; PSF, 2008a). Table 1 contains a comparison between law enforcement line-of-duty deaths [LODD] and law enforcement suicide deaths. Line-of-duty deaths are deaths of law enforcement officers while at work, such as deaths occurring due to accidents, assaults, auto accidents, duty related illness, gunfire, heart attacks, motorcycle accidents, vehicle strikes, vehicle pursuits, and vehicular assaults (ODMP, 2009). Law enforcement suicides are deaths of law enforcement officers by suicide.

Table 1

Line-of-Duty Deaths and Law Enforcement Suicide Deaths from 2004-2009

Year	LOD Deaths	Law Enforcement Suicides	Difference
2004	164	449	285
2005	164	447	285
2006	156	452	299
2007	192	397	208
2008	138	402	278
2009	120		
Total	814	2147	1355
Average	163	429	294

Note: Developed from ODMP, 2004, 2005, 2006, 2007, 2008, 2009 the

National Police Suicide Foundation [PSF], 2008a).

Table 1 is a *living document,* which causes the totals to vary. Data

presented in Table 1 may change, if the result of complications suffered from

in the line-of-duty accidents or complications of suicide attempts prove fatal.

Suicide numbers for 2009 not verified and are not yet available for

publication by the National Police Suicide Foundation (R. Douglas, personal

communication, January 29, 2010). Due to the lack of information available

for law enforcement suicide numbers for 2009, the figures, totals, and

averages are not included in Table 1.

Substance abuse and relationship issues are major contributors of law enforcement suicide (Waters & Ussery, 2007). Excessive alcohol use, also referred to as *choir practice*, among law enforcement officers contributes to relationship problems at home, in the department, and within the community (Crank, 2004; Lejoyeux et al., 2008). Choir practice is the excessive consumption of alcohol by law enforcement officers as a way to counteract stress and to increase the bonding process with fellow officers (Crank, 2004).

Officers suffering from psychiatric disorders such as depression often mask outward symptoms of mental illness through the consumption of prescription and non-prescription drugs and alcohol (Kelly & Martin, 2006). Depression is the most common psychiatric disorder associated with suicide (Andrew, 2008; Bertolote, Fleischmann, De Leo, & Wasserman, 2004). Approximately 60 - 90% of individuals nationwide who commit suicide have a diagnosis of depression ("Treating depression," 2009, p. 580). Although depression is treatable, the condition is difficult to diagnose because depression mimics signs and symptoms of other conditions, such as alcohol abuse, grief, fatigue, fibromyalgia, and Post Traumatic Stress Disorder (PTSD) (Andrew, 2008; Cross & Ashley, 2004; "Misdiagnosis of depression," 2009). Atypical manifestations of depression often mask the underlying disease. The attending physician misses the masked signs and symptoms, and the patient experiencing depression goes undiagnosed. Self-medication increases the likelihood of masking the symptoms of depression, which goes unnoticed by spouses, family members, colleagues, and medical personnel (De Paulo & Horvitz, 2002; O'Hara & Violanti, 2009; Tuck, 2009). Moreover, the signs and symptoms associated with depression are more difficult to diagnose when depressed individuals self-medicate with prescription and non-prescription drugs and alcohol.

Law enforcement officers frequently commit suicide when they become depressed (Andrew, 2008). Waters and Ussery (2007) reported that peer support systems, such as debriefings and visits with departmental chaplains, helped law enforcement officers overcome the sense of isolation and hopelessness due to depression. The problem is that depressed officers lack appropriate support systems, resulting in increased use of alcohol and isolation from peers. Administrators are unsure how to address effectively difficult personal situations (Kelley, 2005; Waters & Ussery, 2007). Because of the lack of mental health training, officers do not know the significance of depression and suicide; they do not know how to approach their leaders with personal problems and many suffer in silence (Kelley, 2005; Violanti, 2003, as cited in Hackett & Violanti).

Issues of trust and occupational segmentation exist between line officers and administration (Crank, 2004). Line officers and administration have separate cultural norms and those individuals conducting administrative duties try to manage through coercion. Cultural and operational differences exist between line officers and administration, and these differences become more apparent over time, causing line officers to mistrust individuals in administration (Crank, 2004).

According to Crank, (2004) the number one stressor for law enforcement officers is organizational administration. Law enforcement leadership "represents a crucial determinant of police organizational efficacy" (Schafer, 2008, p. 13). Leadership can also be problematic by micro-managing departments. Micro managing occurs when administrators do not allow officers to become leaders by using their own discretion. Schafer (2008) explained that for line officers to become leaders, officers must be allowed to encounter failure. Failure allows administrators to demonstrate they are not only concerned with officers' personal and professional development, but that they trust the judgment and discretion of the officers they hired. The inability for officers to use discretion can lead to increased levels of stress and can cause officers to question their ability to use discretion (Schafer, 2008).

Exhibiting or concealing signs of increased stress can contribute to the declining mental function of officers, placing them and their departments in danger (Tuck, 2009). Departments face liability for negative officer contact, excessive use-of-force, and substance abuse on and off duty by officers (Kappeler, 1999; Kappeler, Sluder, & Alpert, 1998). Law enforcement administrators are "typically more concerned with deviance and dysfunction than with health and resilience" (Kelley, 2005, p. 7). According to Kelley, law enforcement administrators are more likely to be concerned with deviance and dysfunction when they and educators take the mental health of officers for granted. Waters and Ussery (2007) noted that although numerous preventative treatment programs focusing on officer stress and mental health are available to law enforcement, many officers do not use the programs because of strong cultural influences shrouding mental health. Officers with declining mental function often self-medicate with prescription and non-prescription drugs and alcohol. Kelley linked relationship problems at work and home, physical illness, accidents on the job, a lack of group cohesion, and clinical depression to issues of self-medication. For law enforcement personnel to manage at optimal mental functioning, a positive mental outlook, that acknowledges and overcomes past feelings formerly defined as taboo within the law enforcement community, is necessary (Blum, 2000). According to Diamond (2003), there was "no reason to expect law enforcement officers possess any special immunity from this disease [clinical depression], or its fatal consequence" (p. 55).

Statement of the Problem

The general problem is that suicide is the leading cause of death for law enforcement officers in the United States (Kelly & Martin, 2006; PSF, 2008; Violanti, 2007). Occupational subcultures, such as law enforcement, exhibit increased levels of stress, trauma, and identifiable social roles, which further compound the risk of suicide (Burke & Mikkelsen, 2007; Kelley, 2005; Violanti, Castellano, O'Rourke, & Paton, 2006). The specific problem is that law enforcement suicide in the United States occurs at a rate of seven times the rate of suicides within the general population (Tate, 2004). Researchers have found links between the increased number of officer suicides, alcohol abuse, relationship issues, isolation from peers, depression, and the availability of handguns (Kelly & Martin, 2006; Violanti, 2007; Waters & Ussery, 2007). Law enforcement suicide occurs at a rate of 14 to 28 deaths per 100,000, compared to 12 deaths per 100,000 within the general population (PSF, 2008a). A qualitative phenomenological study was conducted to elicit perceptions and the lived experiences of law enforcement officers from municipal, county, and federal law enforcement agencies concerning the impact of mental health training on the incidence of law enforcement suicide.

Purpose of the Study

The purpose of the study was to explore the lived experiences of law enforcement officers concerning perceptions of care by administrators and peers and the influence of mental health training on the incidence of officer suicide. A qualitative method allows for the collection of information and data, which comes in many forms (i.e. symbols, words, themes, and meanings) (Neuman, 2005). The phenomenological design may assist in uncovering officer perceptions about the influence of mental health training on dealing with difficult personal situations. Moustakas acknowledged the importance of understanding perception in phenomenological research in order to understand the phenomenon being researched.

Data collection consisted of an individual interview in which study participants are asked 7 demographic and 18 interview questions. The intimate setting allows for privacy, which may contribute to participant honesty. Perception of the law enforcement officers involved in the study may provide insight and knowledge of their lived experiences contributing to potential issues of mental health and mental health training, which provides mental stability to individuals with increased levels of stress and in times where personal safety is compromised (Moustakas, 1994). Moustakas acknowledged the importance of understanding perception in phenomenological research in order to understand the phenomenon being researched.

Uncovering the knowledge, experiences, and perceptions of law enforcement officers about the influence of mental health training on difficult issues, may provide administration insight regarding the nature of training that could reduce the incidence of suicide among law enforcement officers. Explored were the perceptions of 20 White, male law enforcement officers from Madison and Saint Clair Counties in Illinois, and Saint Louis County, Missouri. White, male law enforcement officers were appropriate for the study because the CDC (2005) classified White males as a high-risk population for increased rate of suicide. White males are four times more likely to commit suicide than their White female counterparts are and twice as likely to commit suicide as Black males (CDC, 2005).

Significance of the Problem

Law enforcement is a dangerous occupation exposing officers daily to harmful and traumatic events (Kelley, 2005; Violanti, Castellano, O'Rourke, & Paton, 2006). Continuous exposure to stressful and traumatic events puts officers at risk for mental health issues such as depression (Violanti, 2008). Officers suffering from depression may lose the ability to rationalize, causing lapses in judgment (Kelley, 2005). The significance of the study was twofold. First, study results may contribute to a better understanding of mental health issues, by providing officers appropriate alternatives if they experience difficult personal situations. Second, the contributions made to understanding mental health issues may lead to a reduction in the number of law enforcement suicides.

Academy training is the major component separating law enforcement officers from non-law enforcement officers (Kelley, 2005). Academy training produces a foundation of self-awareness, self-empowerment, capability, and competency of predetermined skill sets necessary for officer survival (Clement, Hough, & Jones, 2007). Training increases skill sets, while decreasing preconceived notions, prejudices, and stigmas associated with specific situations (Penn & Couture, 2002). Training, rituals, and culture establishes precedence with new recruits in the police officer academy (Crank 2004). Thus, training on difficult issues may have a deeper, more lasting effect if taught in the academy setting (Kelly & Martin, 2006). Knowledge and skills taught in the academy setting focus on officer survival (i.e., firearms training, defensive tactics, hand-to-hand combat) (Kelley, 2005), and officer "deviance and dysfunction" (Kelley, 2005, p. 7). Familiarizing recruits with the issues that are taking the lives of officers may provide awareness within the law enforcement community about the number one killer of law enforcement officers, suicide (Kelly & Martin, 2006). According to Kelley (2005), ignorance remained the number one reason law enforcement administrators and educators failed to train and educate law enforcement on issues of mental health.

Training programs dealing with mental health issues and mental illness are limited in many law enforcement academy settings (Cooper, McLearen, & Zapf, 2004; Kelley, 2005). Historically, stigma attached to mental illness caused law enforcement personnel to label individuals suffering from mental health issues as problematic and incapable of receiving adequate assistance. A lack of empathy and consideration for individuals suffering from mental health issues is often the result of inadequate training and education about mental illness, and the belief suicide is a taboo topic (Shneidman, 1996), and a lack of support between law enforcement personnel and outside mental health agencies (Cooper et al., 2004; Wells & Schafer, 2006).

Law enforcement culture influences officers' feelings, actions, and behaviors during difficult circumstances (Crank, 2004; Jaramillo, Nixon, & Sams, 2005; Waters & Ussery, 2007). Law enforcement culture is a set of unspoken rules, often taking precedence in the absence of departmental policy and procedure (Crank, 2004). Officers learn the importance of training through real life experiences (Clement et al., 2007; Kelly & Martin, 2006). Researchers accredited reducing departmental liability and providing lifesaving skills to training (Kelley, 2005; Waters & Ussery, 2007).

Significance to the Study to Leadership

The research results may prove useful to law enforcement administrators by providing insight about officer perceptions of care concerning difficult law enforcement issues and whether there is adequate training available to effectively deal with difficulties facing police department's nationwide (i.e., depression, stress, mental illness, and law enforcement suicide). Mandatory preventative training programs may reduce the stigma associated with mental illness and suicide within law enforcement ranks, while possibly reducing the number of yearly officer suicides. Acknowledgment of officer suicide by law enforcement administration allows for the distribution of governmental funding for training on difficult issues (Kelley, 2005). The results of the study may benefit current and future law enforcement administrators who may encounter officers dealing with difficult situations or officers exhibiting the signs and symptoms of depression and mental illness. Law enforcement administrators must understand the importance of changing officer perceptions about stigma attached to issues of mental health, by helping break down barriers in law enforcement culture (Overton & Medina, 2008; Violanti, Castellano, O'Rourke, & Paton, 2006).

Between 2004 and 2008, LODD in the United States totaled 814 (ODMP, 2004, 2005, 2006, 2007, 2008). Reported law enforcement suicides in the United States during the same period totaled 2,147 (O. Ramos, personal communication, May 20, 2009). Nationwide, law enforcement suicides averaged an increase of 263% over LODD from

2004-2008 (see Table 1). According to Douglas (personal communication, July 21, 2009), Director of the PSF, if jumbo jets fell out of the sky at a rate comparable to yearly law enforcement suicides, the Federal Aviation Administration [FAA] would ground jumbo jets in order to determine what was causing the crashes.

The incidence of law enforcement suicide is a topic many law enforcement administrators would rather not discuss (Kelley, 2005). In an attempt to conceal the occurrence of officer suicide, many deaths are misclassified, misrepresented, or concealed (Violanti, 2007). According to Violanti (2007), approximately 20% of law enforcement suicides were misclassified (p. 14). The misclassification, misrepresentation, and concealment of officer suicide by law enforcement administration cause a lack of attention about officer suicide and contribute to a lack of governmental funding for Police Suicide Awareness [PSA] training (Douglas, 1997).

Nature of the Study

The focus of qualitative research is on meanings and experiences that people place on phenomena within a specific social content (Kirk & Miller, 1986; Moustakas, 1994), and includes "research about persons' lives, stories, behavior, but also about occupational functioning, social movements, or interactional relationships" (Strauss & Corbin, 1990, p. 17). Qualitative research often originates out of a lack of literature (Moustakas, 1994). The focus of qualitative methods is on broad, open-ended questions, seeking perspective and insight into the phenomenon being investigated (Neuman, 2005). The focus of the current study was on the perceptions of the participants and the wealth of information participants provided, making a qualitative method appropriate for the proposed study.

The use of qualitative research allows a researcher to reflect through abstract forms of thinking, while maintaining a safe distance from the participant and the phenomenon being studied (Moustakas, 1994). All interviews in the current study were conducted using the modified van Kaam method introduced by Moustakas. The modified van Kaam method introduced by Moustakas includes a semi-structured interview process with audio-recorded interviews. The use of the software program NVivo® assisted in extracting common themes and perceptions from the research population. The use of NVivo® "removes many of the manual tasks associated with analysis, like classifying, sorting and arranging information, so more time exists to explore trends, build and test theories and ultimately arrive at answers to questions" (QSR International, 2007, para. 2).

A phenomenological design was appropriate for the research study because with a phenomenological approach participant perceptions could be used to challenge common beliefs and misconceptions about the phenomenon being researched (Kirk & Miller, 1986; Moustakas, 1994). The use of a phenomenological research design allows for the extraction of individual perceptions, producing a more meaningful explanation of common daily experiences (van Manen, 1990). Phenomenology lacks the possibility of producing effective or explainable theory, but rather, it begins to produce insight about the phenomena (van Manen, 1990). Van Manen explained phenomenology as "the systematic attempt to uncover and describe the structures, the internal meaning structures, of the lived experience" (p. 10). Phenomenology is the intentional account of how things appear to the individual, rather than the collective (Moustakas, 1994; Sokolowski, 2007). Preconceived notions and individual beliefs occur at the time of exposure. Once exposure occurs, preconceived notions and beliefs become the individual reality

(Sokolowski, 2007). A phenomenon consists of three formal structures: (a) the structure of 'parts and wholes," (b) the structure to "identity in a manifold" (Sokolowski, 2007, p. 22), and (c) the structures of the "presence and absence" (Sokolowski, 2007, p. 22).

Examined in the qualitative phenomenological study were the perceptions and lived experiences of 20 White, male police officers within Madison and Saint Clair Counties in Illinois and Saint Louis County, Missouri, concerning the influence of mental health training on the incidence of law enforcement suicide. Uncovering officer perceptions concerning the role of mental health training among law enforcement officers may facilitate the development of new perspectives and insight into the incidence of law enforcement officer suicide. Officer perceptions were the focus of the study and may provide insight to administrators and officers about the concerns regarding perceptions of care and the reasons why some officers see suicide as an option, while others do not.

The population included White, male law enforcement officers within municipal, county, and federal law enforcement agencies in Madison and Saint Clair Counties in Illinois, and Saint Louis County, Missouri. According to the CDC (2005), White males reflected the segment of the population declared high risk for suicide. Eligible agencies included departments with at least 10 sworn full-time officers. Eligible officers were sworn full-time officers selected from eligible departments, possessing a minimum of 5 years full-time law enforcement service.

A point-of-contact within each eligible participating law enforcement agency chose study participants randomly. The selected males had initial law enforcement academy training, and might have been exposed to additional types of job training. The chances of receiving some type of PSA training by the participants increased with time in the law enforcement environment. Exposure to law enforcement culture and the realities of law enforcement work often expose officers to the realities of life and death within the first few years on the force (Crank, 2004).

Research Questions

According to Neuman (2005), qualitative research was guided by a general research question about the phenomenon being researched. Within the context of the current study, the primary focus was prevention of law enforcement suicide. The research question for the current study was: *What are the lived experiences and perceptions of law enforcement officers concerning the effects of training and perceptions of care on the incidence of suicide among law enforcement officers?*

Officer perceptions were addressed in the research questions regarding mental health training and officer assumptions about training's role on the incidence of law enforcement suicide. Participant responses may produce a better understanding of the impacts of perceived care and training on difficult issues. Uncovered in the research may be an effective solution, which may assist in reducing or eliminating officer suicide. The importance of the study was to uncover officer perceptions and assumptions about possible benefits of mental health training and perceptions of care by peers and administrators within their departments.

Theoretical Framework

The focus of the theoretical framework for the study was on suicide theories (Durkheim, 1979; & Linehan, 1986; Freud, 1935; Shneidman and Farberow, 1957) and also on the role of perceptions in creating reality. "Suicide has been variously called the most daring, most courageous, most generous way to die (*and* its opposite, most cowardly way to die), but, a priori, … is not the most adaptive mode of death in an evolutionary sense" (Shneidman, 1985, p. 37). Examining suicide theory is important, not to decide whether the act is courageous or cowardly, but to examine possible perceptions leading to suicide and motivations for suicide (Hackett & Violanti, 2003; Shneidman, 1985).

Freud focused on the individuals desire to die. Freud termed this desire to die the *death instinct* (Boeree, 2006). The death instinct represents itself as a way out. Individuals unable to achieve goals and personal desires may revert to thoughts of death if success is unattainable (Boeree, 2006). The inability to succeed, or the perception of the inability to succeed, can lead to an inward display of hostility and aggression (Waters & Ussery, 2007). The inability to succeed can lead to inner turmoil. Suicide and homicide often result due to the internalization of negative emotion and turmoil (Boeree, 2006).

Shown in the comparative model of suicide proposed by Shneidman and Farberow (1957), individuals constantly compared themselves to others. Represented in the Shneidman and Farberow model is a perception of individual reality. The Shneidman and Farberow theory of suicide resembles the theory presented by Durkheim (1979), in which individuals seek social acceptance. The inability to integrate socially leads to breakdowns in relationships, often resulting in isolation and depression. Individuals suffering from depression have increased risks for "abnormally" driven types of behaviors (De Paulo & Horvitz, 2002, p. 120). De Paulo and Horvitz (2002) defined abnormally driven types of behaviors as behaviors, which are the result of negative consequences and destructive outcomes of such behaviors (i.e. chemical dependence, addiction, and self-injury). Individuals suffering from depression coupled with abnormally driven and destructive behaviors increase one's chances of suicide (De Paulo & Horvitz, 2002; Kelly & Martin, 2006; Waters & Ussery, 2007).

Durkheim (1979) focused on the internal and external environmental factors, influencing human behavior, believing suicide was a social factor, in which real or perceived caused society to place expectations on all individuals. Humans are social creatures whom expect a sense of belonging to some type of social identity (Durkheim, 1979). Individuals lacking the ability to integrate socially have increased risks of suicide (Durkheim, 1979). A lack of social integration increases isolation, resulting in depression, which contributes to increased risk of suicide and suicidal behavior (Durkheim, 1979).

Examined in the theory of suicide presented by Linehan (1993) were components of dysfunctional behavior. Linehan (1993) believed individuals completed suicide because they lacked skills that may have allowed them to choose options that are more appropriate. Individuals committing suicide possessed emotions well outside the range considered normal and acceptable (Linehan, 1986, 1993; Putnam & Silk, 2005). Linehan believed individuals possessing unacceptable range of emotion, especially in early childhood, were less able to form successful adult relationships (Linehan, 1993). The inability to form successful adult relationships can lead to deficient support systems, increasing the susceptibility of suicide (Linehan, 1986, 1993). Once an individual commits suicide, the possibility to understand fully the motives or reasons behind the act is seemingly impossible (Jamison, 1999). The taking of an individual's own life does not appear logical, but logic and perception may be clouded by physical or emotional impairments such as mental illness and substance abuse. Physical and emotional impairments may cause an individual to see suicide as a logical option (Jamison, 1999).

The existence of such impairments does not minimize the idea that human perception allows for the creation of individual reality through the construction of meaning (Jamison, 1999). As indicated in Freud's theory of suicide, individuals unable to attain personal goals often display a gamut of emotions. The problem remains whether the individual is operating in reality or perception. Individuals may perceive they do not possess adequate support systems, blurring the line between perception and reality.

Knowledge acquisition occurs through sensation and perception (Ott, 1996). Kuhn (1996) explained "[w]hat a man sees depends both upon what he looks at and also upon what his previous visual-conception experience has taught him to see . . . the absence of such training there can only be . . . 'a bloomin' buzzin' confusion' " (p. 113). According to Kotler and Keller (2006), perception is a process in which the "individual selects, organizes, and interprets information inputs to create a meaningful picture of the world" (p. 285). Training changes the information selected, organized, and ultimately interpreted, in-turn changing perceptions, behaviors, and outcomes (Kotler & Keller, 2006). The implementation of training on difficult issues may increase officer knowledge base about mental health issues, while decreasing preconceived notions and stigmas.

Definition of Terms

The following section is comprised of definitions, which were used in the dissertation. Terms have different definitions to the public and the law enforcement community. For the purpose of the study, the following definitions were used:

Brotherhood: Brotherhood refers to the solidarity between the men and women in blue. Brotherhood is a form of honor and solidarity to the blue culture engaging cohesiveness, loyalty, and esprit-de-corps (Crank, 2004).

Choir Practice: Choir practice refers to a ritualistic time officer's share drinking, often excessively, as a way to celebrate when roles and rank are leveled (Crank, 2004; McNulty, 1994). Choir practice occurs when officers are off duty.

Code of Silence: The Code of Silence among police officers "is the perception that police officers will never inform on other officers even if that officer is involved in illegal activity" (Hall, 2002, p. 3).

Completed Suicide: Completed suicide is synonymous with suicide; the physical act of taking one's own life (Shneidman, 1985).

Critical Incident Stress (CIS): Critical incident stress is a type of stress resulting from circumstances, which may be overwhelming. Such events are "sudden, powerful events that fall outside the range of ordinary human experiences. Because they happen so abruptly, they can have a strong emotional impact, even on an experienced, well-trained officer" (Kureczka, 1996, para. 7).

Critical Incident Stress Management (CISM): Critical incident stress management is a comprehensive support group interacting with participants to help them deal with the massive emotions caused by stress (Mitchell & Everly, 1993).

Culture: Culture involves "aspects of human cognition and activity that are derived from what we learn as members of society, keeping in mind that one learns a great deal that one is never explicitly taught" (Monaghan & Just, 2000, p. 35).

Line-of-duty death (LODD): A line-of-duty death involves the death of a law enforcement officer while on duty. The types of deaths include "accidental, assault, automobile accident, duty related illness, gunfire, heart attack, motorcycle accident, struck by vehicle, vehicle pursuit, and vehicular assault" (ODMP, 2009, p.1).

Quasi-suicide: A quasi-suicide is an "attempted suicide with less than total lethality" (Shneidman, 1985, p. 17).

Rookie: Rookie is a term used to identify officers with "limited tenure and experience as a police officer" (Henry, 2004, pp. 39-40). Probationary periods for rookie officers can range from 1 to 5 years (Henry, 2004, pp. 39-40).

Suicide Ideation: Suicide ideation includes one's capacity to form or entertain ideas about suicide (American Psychological Association, 2009).

Veteran: A veteran is a term used to describe officers who are no longer on probation (Henry, 2004).

Warrior: A warrior is an individual within a department who understand the relationship between the department and the militaristic persona, in which the police are soldiers involved in a war against the streets (Crank, 2004).

Assumptions

For the purpose of the study, it was assumed participants were honest. Participant honesty is subjective, in that officer perception of events or situations may not mirror the actuality of the event. Quinn (2005) explained officers form a brotherhood and are protected by the Code of Silence, and through the Code of Silence many officers developed the ability to be deceptive. It is through such deception that the truth becomes less transparent, and the power of the Code of Silence is witnessed. "Omissions, lies, and deception in reports and testimony—when carefully mixed with the truth—become the weapons of choice in the war on crime" (Quinn, 2005, p. 7).

According to Quinn (2005) "the Code of Silence—the singularly most powerful influence on police behavior in the world" (p. 4). Officers may be reluctant about sharing information, sharing honestly, or they may fear giving too much information. Reluctance may be the result of the nature of the topic, the culture of law enforcement, or the possibility participants may know someone who has suffered from mental health issues or has committed suicide (Waters & Ussery, 2007). The assumption was that officers were reluctant to speak about the topic of law enforcement suicide, because law enforcement administrators may not acknowledge suicide within officer ranks (Waters & Ussery, 2007).

The law enforcement culture perpetuates a lack of acknowledgement by administrators concerning officer suicide. Law enforcement culture allows officers and administration to conceal officer suicide by the Code of Silence (Hackett & Violanti, 2003). The Code of Silence is a set of unwritten rules, which include secrecy of questionable behavior by law enforcement officers (Quinn, 2005). Quinn characterized the Code of Silence as *walking with the devil* (p. 25). Walking with the devil defines a mysterious and secretive act practiced by all law enforcement officers at some time in their careers.

Scope, Limitations, and Delimitations

The scope refers to what is contained within the boundaries of the study (Creswell, 2005). A discussion of scope should include the sample size, the method for acquiring data, and the way in which the data will be analyzed. Limitations are threats to internal validity and include the things, which are out of control of the constructed research. Delimitations are threats to external validity and include those things, which the researcher could control, but chooses not to control.

Scope.

The research study included 20 White, male law enforcement officers. This population mirrors the segment of the population declared high-risk for suicide by the CDC (2005). Only sworn or commissioned, full-time, White, male officers from law enforcement agencies within Madison and Saint Clair Counties in Illinois, and Saint Louis County, Missouri, were included. Study participants are selected from departments employing a minimum of 10 full-time officers and each officer is required to have a minimum of 5 years full-time law enforcement experience. By the time 20 participants are interviewed, data saturation should be reached (Neuman, 2005). Data for the study was collected using audio recording equipment, field notes, and interviews implemented using the modified van Kaam method introduced by Moustakas. The collected data was analyzed using the NVivo® software program.

Limitations.

Face-to-face interviews limit participant honesty and time availability. Time availability may cause officers to rush the process in an attempt to finish the interview. Time availability can include personal or work time issues and will be addressed by scheduling appointments at the convenience of officers. Limitations include possible scheduling conflicts due to shift work, overtime, and sensitivity to the research topic. Individuals are highly opinionated, and such opinions may appear in qualitative types of research (Neuman, 2005). Qualitative researchers do not attempt to generalize results;

rather qualitative research provides a distinctive interpretation of the phenomenon (Moustakas, 1994). The lack of literature on law enforcement suicide and the potential misclassification of officer suicides may contribute to a limitation of truthfulness by participants.

Participant reluctance may be contributed to the sensitivity of the topic of law enforcement suicide. Physical and emotional demands placed on officers often perpetuate the minimization of feelings and beliefs as a means of personal protection (Crank, 2004). Over time, the minimization of feelings may inadvertently hinder participant openness. In an attempt to address the minimization of officer feelings, the following steps were taken with all participants to ensure participant openness (a) participants were allowed adequate time to respond to all questions, (b) participants were allowed time to have any questions or concerns answered, (c) participants questions or concerns were addressed, and (d) if for any reason participants requested a break, adequate time was given.

Even though qualitative designs allow for a more abundant interpretation of the phenomenon being researched, such designs also contribute to issues of dependability and trustworthiness of participant responses. The steps taken to mitigate such issues include understanding the limitations of a qualitative design. Participant interpretations of the phenomenon being research are often individualistic and can change over time.

The generalizability of the study refers to the "ability to draw correct inferences from the sample data to other persons, settings, and to past and future situations" (Creswell, 2005, p. 293). Creswell (2005) explained that for external validity or generalizability to be apparent, random selection of participants should occur, or multiple processes should be conducted with numerous participants from the selected population. Generalizability influences the external validity of the research. Random selection does not provide each law enforcement agency with an equal chance of selection; therefore, to increase the generalizability of the study, numerous participants were selected from eligible law enforcement agencies.

Generalizability related to the results of the study and the ability for the results to be applied to a larger population (Neuman, 2005). The generalizability of the current study results to other law enforcement agencies and the general population was limited by the small sample size. Municipal, county, and federal law enforcement agencies are regulated by different jurisdictions, which may contribute to differences in academy training requirements, continuing education requirements, and law enforcement culture (Crank, 2004). The small sample size did not allow for the generalizability to larger populations. Conclusions may be made within the sample population but the conclusions will not be generalizable to other law enforcement personnel or to the general population.

Delimitations.

The focus of the study was on officer perceptions regarding the influence training has on officer suicide. Participants were included if they met eligibility requirements and their department agreed to participate in the study. Individuals meeting study criteria may participate without department approval, as there is no need to illicit permission from these departments. The interviews conducted by individuals choosing to participate without departmental approval was done outside the officers department and while the officer was not on duty. Participants were excluded from further participation in the study if their eligibility status changes. The following participants were excluded from the study: non-law enforcement affiliated personnel, non-Caucasians, females, officers without 5 years full-time law enforcement experience, and those not employed in a law enforcement agency within Madison and Saint Clair Counties in Illinois, and Saint Louis County, Missouri.

The research was limited to the geographical locations of Madison and Saint Clair Counties in Illinois and Saint Louis County, Missouri. The delimitation increases researcher and participant convenience in conducting face-to-face interviews. Only subjects matching the study criteria were chosen. According the CDC (2005), males were four times more likely to complete suicide than females, with White males completing suicide at a higher rate than black males (see also Pegula, 2004; Shneidman & Mandelkorn, 1967).

Summary

Chapter 1 includes information related to the need for a qualitative phenomenological study on the issue of law enforcement suicide and the role suicide and preventative training may have on reducing the number of yearly law enforcement suicides. Suicide is a public health concern of epidemic proportions (CDC, 2005; Satcher, 1999). Increased rates of suicide occur in cultures where suicide is taboo (Shneidman, 1996). The taboo nature of suicide further perpetuates the need for law enforcement to conceal or misclassify officer suicide. The law enforcement community often views officer suicide as a cowardly act, claiming more lives each year than officers killed in the line-of-duty (ODMP, 2009; Violanti & Samuels, 2007).

Two major contributors to law enforcement suicide are substance abuse and relationship issues (Lejoyeux et al., 2008; Violanti, 2007; Waters & Ussery, 2007).

Individuals working in occupations where there are increased levels of stress, traumatic incidents, and identifiable social roles is more susceptibility to suicide (Cross & Ashley, 2004). Law enforcement culture further perpetuates the issue of officer suicide through secrecy, shame, and unwritten rules, known as the Code of Silence (Quinn, 2005). The taboo nature of suicide in the United States leads to increased numbers of individuals suffering silently from depression and to increased numbers of suicide (WHO, 2000). Misrepresentation or misclassification of many law enforcement deaths occurs because officer suicide is taboo (Violanti, 1996; WHO, 2000).

Many law enforcement suicides are misclassified or classified as accidental for reasons of shame and insurance (Violanti, 1996). The lack of acknowledgement by officers, supervisors, and administrators about depression and suicide within law enforcement ranks reinforces a common mindset that suicide and depression are nonexistent within the law enforcement community and do not require training. The misclassification and concealment of suicide-related deaths restricts the disbursement of governmental funding for training and prevention programs (Clark & White, 2003, as cited in Hackett & Violanti; PSF, 2008b).

Chapter 2 begins with an examination of relevant literature concerning theoretical frameworks of suicide, to include Freud, Durkheim, Linehan, and Shneidman, and Farberow. The literature review includes a discussion on law enforcement suicide and the role individual perception and cognitive and behavioral learning theory have on perceptions of suicide. Chapter 2 also includes an in-depth discussion about the ritualistic nature of law enforcement culture and training. The presence of culture may influence law enforcement officials (Crank, 2004). Chapter 2 concludes with a discussion of the possible contributing factors of law enforcement suicide: depression,

mental illness, and a lack of peer support (Waters & Ussery, 2007).

Chapter 2: Review of the Literature

The purpose of the study was to explore the lived experiences of law enforcement officers concerning perceptions of care by administrators and peers and the influence of mental health training on the incidence of officer suicide. Uncovering officer perceptions about the role of mental health training among officers may facilitate the development of an effective training program that would positively affect the phenomenon of suicide among law enforcement officers. The lack of mental health training within law enforcement ranks conveys the message to officers that depression and suicide are not issues of importance or issues defined by leadership as needing such attention (Kelley, 2005; Hackett & Violanti, 2003).

Chapter 2 includes information regarding the literature search process and includes a review of the relevant literature concerning the perceptions of law enforcement officers about training's impact on difficult issues (e.g. depression, mental health, mental illness, and suicide). Contained in the literature review is a discussion of the research and theories concerning cognitive learning theory, behavioral learning theory, perception, law enforcement culture, law enforcement training, and suicide. Chapter 2 concludes with an examination of risk factors of officer suicide, law enforcement as a profession, stress, post-traumatic stress, relationship issues with peers and administration, and maladaptive coping mechanisms (Cross & Ashley, 2004; Violanti, 2007).

Title Searches, Articles, Research Documents, Journal Researched

There are two objectives of a literature search. The first objective is to examine scholarly studies that pertain to suicide theory. The search guided the investigation of law enforcement suicide, depression, post-traumatic stress disorder, sensation, perception, cognitive learning theory, behavioral learning theory, law enforcement training, law enforcement culture, and job stressors of law enforcement. The second objective is to investigate why law enforcement officers commit suicide. The purposes mentioned were the focus of the literature search.

Online and traditional sources supported the research into the literature. The search included scholarly books, referred journal articles, and research documented through the following library Internet search engines: Emerald, EBSCOhost, InfoTrac OneFile, Journals@Ovid, ProQuest, and PsychARTICLES. Also used was Questia, the online library of books and journals, and handouts from the PSF Train-the-Trainer Course. Although not all of the collected literature was applicable for the proposed study, Table 2 includes a summary of the literature searched by categories.

Table 2

Summary of Literature Search by Category Searched

Category Searched	Scholarly Journals and Articles	Doctoral Dissertations	Books	Electronic Web Sites
Behavior theory	9		6	
Cognitive theory	13		9	1
Law enforcement culture	22		18	9
Law enforcement stressors	24		15	6
Law enforcement suicide	12		4	9
Law enforcement training	11		5	2
Mental illness	16		7	6
Suicide	22		23	8

Content searches use key words and phrases to collect as many applicable academic sources as possible. The key words and phrases used to search sources for the proposed study were *depression, firearms availability, law enforcement culture, law enforcement stressors, law enforcement suicide, law enforcement training, mental illness, organizational administration, police suicide, PTSD, stigma, stress, suicide,* and *suicide theory.* Given the infinite nature of the virtual world of literary sources, the search for primary sources is not completely exhaustive. The majority of sources for the research date between 1999 and 2009, except for earlier literature used for a historical perspective.

A search of databases resulted in numerous reference materials in the form of scholarly journals, peer-reviewed articles, and scholarly books. The use of additional search engines and databases provided a compilation of sources and information concerning the statistics available for suicide, suicide rates, and population demographics of suicide. Associations include the American Psychological Association, CDC, Department of Mental Health, Mental Health America, NCHS, National Institute of Mental Health, ODMP, PSF, U.S. Department of Public Health, U.S. Department of Veterans Affairs, U.S. Public Health Service, and the WHO. Suicide is a sensitive and secretive topic, which is taboo in many cultures. There appears to be a lack of current literature on the topic of law enforcement suicide, often caused by the taboo nature of suicide within intricate subcultures, such as law enforcement.

Literature Review

Theoretical elements of the study include (a) perception and knowledge construction, (b) cognitive learning theory, (c) behavioral learning theory, (d) general theories of suicide, (e) stigmatization of mental illness, (f) law enforcement training, (g) law enforcement culture, (h) law enforcement suicide, and (i) risk factors of law enforcement suicide. To understand better why some individuals take their own lives, it is essential to understand the mindset and contributing behaviors resulting in suicide. Individual perception influences whether individuals feel cared for and whether the actual amount of care is appropriate (Durkheim, 1979; Jamison, 1999). Intricate social groups leave many individuals suffering from mental illness or depression to feel stigmatized. Stigmatized individuals are often hesitant to seek assistance (De Paulo & Horvitz, 2002). Stigmatization of mental health issues causes many individuals to suffer in silence, often resulting in depression and suicide (De Paulo & Horvitz, 2002; Perin, 2007).

Stigma attached to suicide in law enforcement causes many suicides to be concealed or misclassified (Violanti, 2007). The secrecy and shame experienced in law enforcement culture perpetuates the concealment of officer suicide (Violanti, 2008). The concealment and misclassification of officer suicide places departments at-risk for additional suicides and liability issues due to inadequate or non-existent training on difficult issues (PSF, 2008b). Law enforcement administrators misclassifying and concealing law enforcement suicides lose essential governmental funding for training on difficult issues (Violanti, 2008).

The act of suicide is perplexing in that the motives for the act are often a mystery. No matter how one chooses to end their life, "suicide is its own: intensely private, unknowable, and terrible" (Jamison, 1999, p. 73). Suicide as a means of death has existed for hundreds of years and does not discriminate within any group, subculture, or society (Jamison, 1999). The decision to end one's life may seem illogical to many, but may appear to the suicidal individual to be the only logical option. According to Jamison (1999):

> There are no simple theories for suicide, nor are they invariable algorithms with which to predict it; certainly no one has ever found a way to heal the hearts or settle the minds of those left behind in its dreadful wake. What we do not know kills. (pp. 18-19)

Perception and Knowledge Construction

Knowledge is acquired through sensation and perception (Curry, Meyer, & McKinney, 2006; Shipley, Johnson, & Hashemi, 2009) through the ability to reason, associate, and learn (Dalkir, 2005). Knowledge affects understanding and discovery

(Yang, 2003). Individual perception builds attachment to the meanings about the world in which we live, which constructs knowledge (Bush, 2006). Individual perception is absorbed through the senses, resulting in individual interpretations of the incoming data (Ott, 1996).

Sensation is a response by the body to stimuli through "sensory preceptors (e.g., eyes, ears, nose, mouth, fingers) to basic stimuli such as light, color, shape or sound" (Curry et al., 2006, p. 28). Individuals using the five senses, or *sensing,* focus on realistic functions, the basis of past occurrences, and personal perceptions (Jung, 1923). *Perception* is the ability to decide which sensations to choose, categorize, or understand (Curry et al., 2006). Perception influences sensory inputs into the body and brain, allowing individuals to employ preconceived thoughts and ideas regarding the relevancy of presented information. The implementation of preconceived ideas becomes beneficial and detrimental in problem solving and training. Jung (1923) explained intuitive individuals possessed more creativity and inspiration because they remain challenged and innovative in their ventures.

Cognitive Learning Theory

Modifications to learning occur when individuals or collectives exhibit change in information processes, the development of mutual understanding, and the elucidation of incidents; this is also known as cognitive learning theory (Crossan, Lane, White, & Djurfldt, 1995; Roy & Novotny, 2000). Crossan et al. further stated, "cognitive theorists . . . assume learning has occurred if there is a change in thought processes (unobservable), even in the absence of adjusted behavior (observable)" (p. 348).

Learning influences knowledge, perceptions, and beliefs (Fiol & Lyles, 1985). Explicit forms of knowledge are described in cognitive learning theory (Yang, 2003).

Explicit knowledge is easily shared with others in the form of hard data (Hicks, Dattero, & Galup, 2007; Yang, 2003). Individuals possessing explicit knowledge are able to rationalize and observe through the detachment of object and subject (Yang, 2003). According to Yang (2003), explicit knowledge is "codified knowledge that identifies true from false in the reality, and "reflects one's intentional and conscious effort to understand reality" (p. 109). Culture is described in terms of explicit knowledge and is identified as a "lifestyle of people . . . ideas, symbols, preferences, and material objects that they share" (Franzoi, 2005, p. 15). Culture involves the sensing of rituals, behaviors, and the structure and training of law enforcement. Appendix A contains a matrix used to compare the contextual, structural, and human aspects of law enforcement rituals, behaviors, and structures within law enforcement culture. The implementation of rituals, behaviors, and structures allow law enforcement culture to exist and to be maintained, but the culture is dependent on the context, structure, and human aspects in order to remain constant (Crank, 2004).

Officers share opinions and ideas about mental illness, including stigmatizations, perceptions, beliefs, and preconceived notions (Violanti, 2008). The ability of understanding to exceed past experiences allows explicit knowledge sharing between officers in an attempt to gain insight and understanding of those who suffer from mental illness. The ability to share insight from culture and training may assist officers to exhibit to peers there is nothing to fear about individuals suffering from mental illness (Kelley, 2007).

Behavioral Theory of Learning

Behavioral theorists suggest humans learn through prompts received from the environment (Roy & Novotny, 2000). The behaviors are observable and measurable (Good & Brophy, 1990). Brown (2006) reported a link between suicidal behavior and environmental factors. Environmental factors witnessed in early childhood influence behavior in adulthood, resulting in "emotional responses, dysfunctional thought patterns, and dysfunctional behavioral repertoires (e.g., through observational learning, classical conditioning, and reinforcement)" (Brown, 2006, p. 92). Behavioral theories of learning include implicit forms of knowledge.

Implicit knowledge is difficult for individuals to share explicitly because acquisition is individually unique (Edmondson, Winslow, Bohmer, & Pisano, 2002). Real knowledge requires justification, and the inability to justify individual meaning from thought is not real knowledge (Edmondson et al., 2002). Implicit knowledge remains undeclared and concealed, only understandable to the individual rather than the collective, as can be seen in culture (Nonaka & Nishiguchi, 2001).

In subcultures, individuals can focus on the collective, rather than individual qualities (Monaghan & Just, 2000). Individuals bring unique cognitive and behavioral experiences to the collective, helping explain why some officer's commit suicide and some do not. One similarity between law enforcement officers is the dangerous and uncertain nature of law enforcement work, leading to increased levels of stress that may have "a strong link to intra-and interpersonal psychological issues" (Woody, 2005, p. 526). Violanti (2007) explained it was "possible that stress, and/or the inability to adequately cope with stress, may play an integral part in police suicide" (p. 55). The inability to cope with compounding stress may leave officers feeling inadequate compared to their peers, fearing rejection and stigmatization if they ask for help.

General Theories of Suicide

Numerous theorists have attempted to explain why people commit suicide. Freud (1935) explained suicide as an individual expression of aggressive behavior. Shneidman and Farberow (1957) examined suicide in the context of comparing man to himself and to others, with indicators of social acceptance. Durkheim (1979) argued suicide resulted from a lack of social integration. Linehan (1993) explained suicide was the process of eliminating pain and suffering, especially in individuals lacking appropriate coping mechanisms. Common to most suicide theories is the implication of pain and continuous disappointment (Jamison, 1999). Individuals choosing suicide as an option to end the pain and disappointment often lack appropriate coping mechanisms, which could save their lives. "Suicide carries in its aftermath a level of confusion and devastation that is, for the most part, beyond description" (Jamison, 1999, p. 24).

Freud's suicide theory.

Freud (1935) deemed suicide an individual expression of hostility and self-destruction. Freud believed all humans have an unconscious desire to die, termed the *death instinct*. Individuals possess an innate desire to fulfill personal wants and needs. The inability to fulfill personal needs or desires, whether internally or externally motivated, leaves individual struggling when disappointment arises (Boeree, 2006; Freud, 1935). The inability or perception of inability to fulfill personal objectives may lead to depression or despair. Outward indicators of depression include delayed thoughts and actions, slumping posture, and less pleasure in previously enjoyed activities (Diggory,

1976). Inward indicators of depression include negative feelings such as hopelessness, sorrow, feelings of worthlessness, and despair (De Paulo & Horvitz, 2002; Diggory, 1976).

The suicide theory developed by Freud (1935) involved research efforts on the area of the brain where memories and trauma were stored. Memory is not merely intriguing, but is essential to all human function. Memory and learning involve physiological and neurological responses (Baddeley, 2004; Klingberg, 2009). Memory and learning occur with the stimulation of sensory sections (i.e., sight, hearing, smell, touch, and taste) of the brain with positive or negative responses or the lack of stimuli (Baddeley, 2004; Klingberg, 2009).

Karlsson and Christianson (2003) explained law enforcement officers witness numerous traumatic incidents, including thoughts of death or injury of officers, killing or injuring others, traffic accidents in which death results, homicides, and suicides. The handling of dead bodies places significant burdens on the psychological health and well-being of emergency workers (Saari & Silver, 2005; Ursano & McCarroll, 1990). The handling of dead bodies, coupled with the perceptions and sensations of the experience appear to shape officer response to the increased levels of stress and trauma of the incident (Ursano & McCarroll, 1990). Law enforcement officials view death as a socialization process, requiring officers to contemplate their mortality (Henry, 1995). Repeated exposure to death and violence by law enforcement personnel leave many trying to forget the incidents. The reality remains, many of the traumatic experiences are stored in the memory.

Memory becomes useful when recalling information stored for future use (Sage, 1984). A relationship exists between memory and learning, and learning and behavior (Klingberg, 2009; Sage, 1984; Terry, 2009). Whether an individual is swimming, riding a bicycle, or conversing with friends; memory and learning must take place. Learning occurs when remembering to lift the head out of the water to breathe while swimming, remembering to peddle the bicycle to keep from falling off, and recalling and remembering the names of friends and acquaintances when conversing (Sage, 1984). The storage of information and the ability to recall information parallels the relationship between memory and learning.

As an innate feature of the human brain, memory allows for the recall of experiences such as assault on a traffic stop, killing someone in the line-of-duty, or losing a brother or sister in blue (Christos, 2003). Memory is a blueprint of how to react if similar incidents occur. The blueprint allows for behavior change and modification. Without the blueprint of the memory, humans would relive many of the same past experiences without modification of reaction, as each action and reaction would be individually unique (Klingberg, 2009). The inability to articulate traumatic memories causes the brain to place single traumatic or terrifying events, or the culmination of a career of tragedy, into the unconscious, which "cannot be explicitly recalled because they are established too heavily in long-term memory" (Ratey, 2002, p. 210).

Problems occur when officers fail to immediately address traumatic events or traumatic events surface when least expected. The officer witnessing such traumatic events may become overwhelmed with the visions of such tragedy through emotion, without articulation of the actual event (Christos, 2003). Incidents are compounded, resulting in increased levels of stress and feelings of hopelessness and despair. If left untreated, the result can be depression, PTSD, and suicide (National Institute of Mental Health [NIMH], 2004; Ratey, 2002).

Numerous signs and symptoms are apparent prior to one committing suicide; however, oftentimes others fail to recognize or choose not to recognize the signs and symptoms (Waters & Ussery, 2007). Law enforcement officers do not talk about their feelings and in a majority of cases will not seek assistance (Waters & Ussery, 2007). Former San Diego police chief Sanders explained, "Cops don't talk about that kind of stuff . . . They either do it. Or they don't" ("Suicide on the Force," 1997, para. 20). Freud's theory makes sense in that through repeated exposure to death and violence, officers are on a path of self-destruction. The perception of law enforcement officers' overshadows the actuality of law enforcement work.

Shneidman and Farberow's suicide theory.

Shneidman and Farberow (1957) examined the logic of suicide within a modern context, focusing on four styles of logic: normal, contaminated, catalogic, and paleologic. "The implication is that if one knew the lethal modes of reasoning and the suppressed premises (or beliefs) that lead to a deadly conclusion, then one might have effective clues to use in the prediction and prevention of suicide" (Shneidman & Farberow, 1957, p. 63). Shneidman and Farberow's theory is similar to Durkheim's theory in which individuals are always seeking social acceptance. A lack of social acceptance within subcultures such as law enforcement may lead to feelings of despair, and possibly suicide (Shneidman & Mandelkorn, 1967). Although suicide may seem illogical, the individual choosing such an act or outcome makes the decision no matter how illogical the thought pattern might seem (Shneidman & Farberow, 1957).

According to Aristotelian standards, normal logic is suitable "before identity can be made, certain conditions have to be satisfied" (Shneidman & Farberow, 1957, p. 64). The personal characteristics of individuals falling within the realms of normal logic include the elderly or widowed. Many elderly and widowed persons suffer from physical or psychological pain. One choosing suicide as a logical option does so to end one's pain. The logical fallacy is explained by ending individual pain through the act of suicide. The act of suicide does not allow the individual to experience the result of anticipated pleasure or anticipated trauma (Shneidman & Farberow, 1957).

The use of normal logic may assist to explain why officers commit suicide, as a way to end the pain or anticipated trauma of the act of suicide (Waters & Ussery, 2007). Law enforcement officers witness numerous traumatic events daily, and the culmination of these stressors can lead to increased stress, resulting in increased alcohol consumption, in an attempt to mask pain (Violanti, 2007; Waters & Ussery, 2007). Increased alcohol use contributes to increased risk for suicide (Violanti, 2007).

Excessive alcohol consumption is common in the police culture (Blackmore, 1978; Reiss, 1971). Alcohol depresses the central nervous system, which lowers inhibitions and affects judgment (Ratey, 2001). Alcohol consumption allows officers to experience a calming effect prior to the act of suicide (Lindsay, 2008). Alcohol contributes to officers experiencing the anticipated calming effect of suicide prior to the act being committed possess a contaminated logic (Shneidman & Farberow, 1957).

Cultural and religious belief systems contain some form of contaminated logic (Shneidman & Farberow, 1957). Contaminated logic is flawed by semantics, in that individuals choosing suicide through the use of contaminated logic believe suicide provides a transition from life to the hereafter, and is used to protect individual and familial reputations (i.e. honor) (Shneidman & Farberow, 1957). Suicidal individuals use contaminated logic to address individual views of death and the role death has on life (Shneidman & Farberow, 1957). The semantics of contaminated logic often contribute to the implications of death. Law enforcement culture instills in officers that suicide is a cowardly act and individuals suffering from depression or mental illness are problematic (Violanti & Samuels, 2007).

Individuals often view themselves through flawed logic and the use of semantics created in relation to the culture in which they belong (Shneidman & Farberow, 1957). Officers experiencing traumatic and stressful events (e.g. overexposure to death, death of a spouse or child, death of a partner, accident scenes, and the everyday stress of law enforcement) may contemplate suicide as an option to end the pain and suffering, or possible shame they may cause their department or family (Violanti, 2003). A survey conducted by the PSF (1998) received a 98% response rate from 500 officers. The officers surveyed explained they would consider suicide a valuable option in the right circumstances. The following list are the top 11 reasons the surveyed officers explained that they would consider suicide a viable option, "death of a spouse or child, loss of a child or spouse through divorce, terminal illness, responsibility for co-workers death, killed someone out of anger, indictment, feeling alone, sexual accusations, loss of job because of conviction of a crime, and being locked up" (Hackett, 2003, p. 8). In an attempt to alleviate the shame and despair; officers may see suicide as a logical option, believing suicide protects the reputation of individuals affected by the officer's actions (Waters & Ussery, 2007). Mental illness, depression, drugs, and alcohol often contribute to logical fallacies in the thought process. Destructive types of logic often result in confusion between individual perceptions and group perceptions. Individuals resorting to self-medication often distort normal logic, resulting in catalogic, which is the confusion of how the individual fits within the group (Shneidman & Farberow, 1957). Individuals suffering from mental illness may experience hallucinations or delusions, resulting in destructive logic. Destructive logic "is destructive not only in the sense that it disregards the classical rules for semantic clarity and formal reasoning but also in that it destroys the logician" (Shneidman & Farberow, 1957, p. 64).

Law enforcement officers are planners and often plan the act of suicide in detail, allowing time for intervention (PSF, 2008b). Suicide is a solution to a problem, and not viewed as an arbitrary act (Shneidman, 1996). By addressing perceptions of learning, culture, and training, this research may provide insight and knowledge about mental health issues facing law enforcement officers. More importantly, the goal is to reach officers before suicide is an option, by providing officers the training solutions necessary to save their lives.

Durkheim's suicide theory.

Durkheim (1979) placed those who commit suicide in two distinct groups: individuals with organic-psychic dispositions and individuals influenced by internal and external environmental factors. Suicide is a social factor in which (real or perceived) members of society place expectations on individuals, further compounding the issue of suicide within intricate social groups and cultures. Durkheim (1979) argued a lack of social integration by individuals increases chances of suicide. Humans are social creatures and must feel as though they are part of a larger group (Maslow, 1943). Individuals lacking social acceptance and bonding experiences inadvertently have higher rates of suicide (Durkheim, 1979).

Law enforcement leaders help officers build unity and solidarity, but officers suffering from depression or mental illness may inadvertently isolate themselves from other officers (Violanti & Samuels, 2007). Officers not suffering perceive those who are suffering from depression and mental illness as outsiders. The isolation of officers suffering from mental health issues places a unique set of standards and expectations on the officers. The lack of training on difficult issues leaves officers confused about how they can overcome feelings of hopelessness and isolation. The inability of officers to overcome the feelings may result in depression, mental illness, or suicide (Kelly & Martin, 2006).

Insanity is not a prerequisite to suicide (Jamison, 1999). Many individuals who commit suicide are sane (Durkheim, 1979; Jamison, 1999). Individuals falling under the canopy of insanity may have no real motive for suicide (due to mental illness and depression) (Durkheim, 1979; Jamison, 1999). Individuals committing suicide voluntarily will more than likely have a motive, such as a pending divorce, loss of a job, the death of a loved one, or the inability to deal with stress and trauma (Durkheim, 1979; Jamison, 1999).

Durkheim (1979) explained:

> To pursue a goal which is by definition unattainable is to condemn oneself to a
> state of perpetual unhappiness . . . man may hope contrary to all reason, and hope
> has its pleasures even when unreasonable. . . but it cannot survive the repeated
> disappointments of experience indefinitely. (p. 248)

Self-medication with drugs and alcohol may alter one's perception of attainability. Individuals suffering from mental illness will often self-medicate to mask pain and suffering. According to Lindsay (2008), law enforcement officers are twice as likely as the general population to abuse alcohol (p. 74). No empirical studies exist concerning the alcohol consumption of law enforcement officers in the United States, resulting in debates about the actual consumption of alcohol by law enforcement (Lindsay, 2008). The consumption of alcohol by law enforcement is widely debated; however many law enforcement administrators indicate alcohol consumption is problematic within law enforcement ranks (Blackmore, 1978; Lindsay, Taylor, & Shelley, 2008). Attempted and completed suicide within law enforcement is often associated with excessive alcohol consumption (Violanti, 2007; Waters & Ussery, 2007). Alcohol consumption, or *choir practice*, is a rite of passage in law enforcement culture (Crank, 2004; Waters & Ussery, 2007). The amount and severity of alcohol use and abuse is highly debated within the law enforcement community (Lindsay, 2008; Violanti, 2007). Self-medication with prescription and non-prescription drugs and alcohol makes recognizing the signs of depression and mental illness difficult for outsiders to see (Kelly & Martin, 2006; Violanti, 2007).

Linehan's suicide theory.

Linehan (1993) addressed suicide through the basis of dysfunctional types of behaviors. Linehan explained suicide in the minds of certain individuals appeared to be the only way to end suffering. Linehan (1995) speculated suicide was, in part, due to the lack of skills deemed necessary to provide appropriate options. A lack of training within the law enforcement community on mental health issues may leave officers unprepared for the challenges they may face.

Suicide usually does not have one single cause, rather a variety of causes ultimately lead to a person committing suicide. Suicide is complex phenomenon, in which individuals demonstrate different types of behaviors, such as emotion dysregulation (Linehan, 1995; Violanti, 2007). Emotion dysregulation is variations in mood classified as outside acceptable emotional response (Putnam & Silk, 2005). Brown (2006) explained the "suicidal person is the product of a biological vulnerability to emotion dysregulation and harmful childhood environments" (p. 92).

The environment and events within the environment can initiate a chain reaction of dysfunctional thoughts, motions, and negative behaviors (Linehan, 1993, 1995). The environmental role in the triggering aspect of emotions and cognitions is not a starting point for suicidal behavior; rather this is a triggering mechanism to dysfunctional thought patterns and behaviors from previous exposure (Linehan, 1993). Oftentimes, environmental conditions reinforce or reactivate dysfunctional thoughts and behaviors. Common beliefs and values about officers who commit suicide and about individuals suffering from mental illness are reinforced in the law enforcement culture. In the law enforcement culture, the need for solidarity is emphasized by singling out individuals who do not share cultural values and beliefs (Crank, 2004; Quinn, 2005).

The environment reinforces vicious cycles of crisis (Brown, 2006). Individuals suffering from emotional dysregulation are so beyond the normal range of emotional stability that they lack basic problem-solving skills. Emotionally unstable individuals lacking effective support systems are unable to solve problems. Environmental triggers can cause maladaptive coping mechanisms, such as substance abuse as a way to deal with erratic emotions (Linehan, 1995). Deficient and nonexistent support systems are associated with suicide and suicidal behavior (Linehan, 1986). Individuals suffering from emotional dysregulation present themselves as hostile and unapproachable, causing individuals who were previously seen as support systems to distance themselves. Isolation often results in the misclassification of the signs of depression, suicidal behavior, and suicide ideation.

Many suicidal individuals lack adequate support systems because they do not have the communication skills necessary to ask for things they need, often resulting in increased isolation from peers (Brown, 2006). In the law enforcement culture, officers are problem solvers, not problem causers. The invalidation of appropriate responses to behaviors in childhood can lead to the concealment of all emotion, causing confusion about the appropriateness of emotions and causing individuals to address issues internally rather than externally. In the law enforcement culture, officer feelings and emotions are invalidated (Crank, 2004). It is difficult to detect the signs and symptoms of suicidal behavior, suicidal thoughts, mental illness, and depression in individuals suffering from mental illness or in individuals who self-medicate (Linehan, 1995).

A relationship exists between exposure to childhood trauma and the increased risks for chronic fatigue and depression (Heim et al., 2009). Individuals suffering from inner turmoil are *grief-phobic* (Brown, 2006, p. 95). Flawed beliefs about character and weakness are reinforced when individuals are unable to grieve appropriately. In the law enforcement culture, officers who commit suicide are viewed as weak. Belief systems reinforce perceptions about officer suicide through a lack of attendance at funerals of law enforcement officers who commit suicide, a lack of acknowledgement by administration of the cause of death, and the concealment and misclassification of law enforcement suicides (Hackett & Violanti, 2003). A lack of grieving occurs for officers who commit suicide. Officers who commit suicide are symbolically removed from the rank of peers, distancing the dead from the living. Individuals suffering from grief phobias become overwhelmed because of their inability to control the over flow of emotions. The inability to control emotions, or to use acceptable coping mechanisms, leaves individuals struggling internally, causing increased levels of stress, depression, and suicide (Brown, 2006).

Jamison (1999) stated "[t]here are no simple theories for suicide, nor are there invariable algorithms with which to predict it; certainly, no one has ever found a way to heal the hearts or settle the minds of those left behind in its dreadful wake" (p. 19). Numerous theories exist that contain insight into the reasons why some individuals commit suicide; however, these theories focus on psychological forms of pain and the differences between one's reality and one's perception of reality. It appears individual perception plays a much larger role in uncovering individual motives for suicide.

Jamison (1999) explained:

> We know . . . a great deal about the underlying conditions that predispose an
> individual to kill himself—heredity, severe mental illness, an impulsive or violent
> temperament . . . or circumstances in life that interact in a particularly deadly way
> with these predisposing vulnerabilities: romantic failures or upheavals; economic
> and job setbacks; confrontations with the law; terminal or debilitating illnesses;
> situations that cause great shame, or are perceived as such; the injudicious use of
> alcohol or drugs. (p. 19)

The mindset of a person suffering from mental health issues can affect a person's
ability to distinguish between perception and reality (Jamison, 1999). Declining mental
function, erratic and changing personal temperament, increased isolation from peers, a
lack of support systems, and the abuse of drugs and alcohol seem to perpetuate the
internal struggle between perception and reality (Jamison, 1999), and can adversely affect
individual sensation and perception, which in-turn influences individual reality (Ott,
1996).

Stigmatization of Mental Illness

Stigmatization "refers to the process by which people who lack a certain trait
denigrate people who possess it, thus leading to individual differences in social
interaction" (Piner & Kahle, 1984, p. 805). Stigmatization is used as a means of creating
cohesion among individuals considered insiders (Arboleda-Florez & Sartorius, 2008;
Falk, 2001). Approximately 30 thousand individuals take their own lives each year in the
United States (De Paulo, 2002, p. 132). The number of completed suicides may be much
higher due to the stigmatization associated with suicide; many groups fail to acknowledge

such deaths, or choose to conceal such deaths, to spare the family and friend's undue grief and shame (De Paulo, 2002). Individual and group belief systems, values, the media and the law, assist in perpetuating the stigma associated with suicide (De Paulo, 2002; Sales & Kahle, 1980).

Stigmatization has long-lasting effects on labeled individuals, even after successful treatment is sought (Overton & Medina, 2008; Sales & Kahle, 1980). Individuals suffering from mental illness suffer from stigmatization at a much greater rate than any other group (WHO, 2009). Approximately 26% of adults (18 and older) nationwide suffer from at least one mental disorder in any given year (NIMH, 2009, p. 1). Mental illness is a "disease that causes mild to severe disturbances in thinking, perception, and behavior" (Mental Health America [MHA], 2009, para. 8). Stigmatization is the single largest detriment facing individuals wishing to seek mental health assistance (Department of Mental Health [DMH], 2006). The social stigmatization attached to individuals suffering from mental illness often results in the individuals viewed as unpredictable and violent. The truth remains individuals suffering from mental illnesses are more often victims than victimizers (Chamberlain, 2000). Reducing the stigmatization of mental illness will allow those suffering in silence to seek assistance and to seek assistance sooner.

According to De Paulo and Horvitz (2002), "attempts to destigmatize suicide . . . have generally proven unhelpful" (p. 149). De Paulo & Horvitz (2002) explained it is far easier and far more effective to educate and train on the signs and symptoms of depression, than on the after effects of untreated depression, resulting in suicide or quasi-suicide. Individuals should be proactive about destigmatization, focusing on those suffering from mental illness and the importance of seeking assistance, rather than being reactive about the destigmatization of suicide (De Paulo & Horvitz, 2002). When suicide is destigmatized, individuals become more understanding of the choice some make to end their lives. Training, behavior modification, and knowledge acquisition reduce the stigmatization of mental illness (USPHS, n.d.).

Law Enforcement Training

Law enforcement training prepares officers for the challenges they may face in the line-of-duty. In 2005, the average cost of initial law enforcement academy training contracted out, municipal, and technical school academies) was $17,300 per recruit (Scott, 2005). The amount allotted depends largely on departmental budgets and the issuance of governmental grants (Scott, 2005). According to Douglas (2009), Director of the PSF, the cost of the PSA training sponsored by the PSF is $600 to $4,600 per session (personal communication, May 13, 2009). The cost of PSA training varies by department size and the length of training. Of the 18,000 law enforcement agencies nationwide, fewer than 2%, or 360 agencies, offer any form of PSA training (PSF, 2008b).

While the number of lives saved by PSA training is unknown, the lack of training is apparent in the high number of annual law enforcement suicides (Waters & Ussery, 2007). The benefit of additional preventative measures appears to outweigh the cost of additional training by increasing awareness and involvement, while reducing burnout and stress (PSF, 2008a; Waters & Ussery, 2007). Law enforcement officials invest large amounts of time and money into the training and development of law enforcement recruits. For investments to benefit the agency, trained officers must remain with the hiring department for a specified amount of time after initial academy training.

According to Sipkoff (2006), depression is the leading cause of lost productivity in the workplace, totaling $51.5 billion annually (p. 4), with the cost of treating depression totaling $26.1 billion (Sipkoff, 2006, p. 4). According to the Bureau of Justice Statistics (2009), approximately 18,000 law enforcement agencies exist nationwide contributing to over 800,000 full-time sworn law enforcement officers (para. 3). Monetary loss due to workplace productivity far exceeds the cost of PSA training.

Law enforcement training increases officer skill competency, knowledge, and accuracy, while reducing liability, stigmatization, and preconceived notions about the topics of discussion (Crank, 2004; Kelley, 2005). Officer survival training includes a physical component of the protection of police officers through the designation of the duty weapon, the bulletproof vest, physical and reality-based training (i.e. physical armor) (Crank, 2004). Psychological aspects of law enforcement include addressing issues officers may face when required to use lethal force, dealing with trauma, and stress. However, there appears to be a lack of training (i.e. psychological armor) on difficult issues such as mental health, mental illness, depression, and suicide, faced by officers (Kelley, 2005).

A lack of training for officers on dealing with difficult issues, coupled with surmounting stress, can cause officers to revert to maladaptive coping mechanisms (Violanti & Samuels, 2007). Maladaptive coping mechanisms include the consumption of alcohol and prescription or non-prescription drugs in an attempt to conceal emotional vulnerabilities from others and to stop the pain (Cross & Ashley, 2004; Hackett & Violanti, 2003; Waters & Ussery, 2007). Maladaptive coping mechanisms mask the signs and symptoms of prolonged exposure to stress, PTSD, mental illness, and depression, further isolating officers from reality and their peers (Hackett, 2003). To end the pain, many officers self medicate resulting in isolation through negative actions and attitudes toward peers.

Law enforcement is a stressful occupation (Liberman, Best, Metzler, Weiss, & Marmar, 2002; Kelley, 2005; Waters & Ussery, 2007). The stress is due in part to "shift work, pending retirement, negative public perceptions, unsupportive management, and physical ailments" (Perin, 2007, p. 12). Stress is individually exclusive and biased, based on individual perceptions, past experiences, and genetic factors (Violanti, 2005). Liberman et al. classified stress as physical, real, or perceived. The two major stressors for law enforcement include exposure to critical incidents and stress attributed to the routine nature of law enforcement (Liberman et al., 2002). Due to increased levels of stress in law enforcement, officers must be mentally sound. The compromise of mental functioning in law enforcement officers can cause officers to "lose touch with common sense and resilience they need to minimize stress, enjoy their work, and operate at peak performance" (Kelley, 2005, pp. 6-7). Emotional scars left behind stressful and traumatic events often present themselves long after the physical wounds are healed (Blum, 2000).

Law enforcement personnel often view individuals suffering from mental illness as problematic and weak (Waters & Ussery, 2007). According to Waters and Ussery, law enforcement views are due in part to a lack of training about mental illness and a lack of constructive relationships between mental health professionals and law enforcement. Officers often label the mentally ill as troublesome because mentally ill individuals often lack an understanding of the motives behind law enforcement contact, in-turn resulting in resistance from many mentally ill individuals. Individuals possessing authority over the mentally ill are in positions of power and influence, which may contribute to the manipulation of these individuals (Waters & Ussery, 2007). Law enforcement training, "overwhelming emphasizes the defects and deficiencies in people, groups, and institutions, highlighting the products of poor mental health and the theories that attempt to explain them" (Kelley, 2005, p. 7). Compliance by mentally ill individuals may be difficult or non-existent, leading to increased stress for law enforcement (Waters & Ussery, 2007).

Officers believe mental health issues are nonexistent within law enforcement ranks and are not discussed (Douglas, 1997). The lack of training on difficult issues, coupled with stigma attached to mental illness, leaves many officers suffering silently. Unaddressed mental illness in the workplace may lead to a breakdown in healthy occupational boundaries, decreased morale, low productivity, increased sick time, suicide, and homicide (Waters & Ussery, 2007). Individuals suffering from mental illness have much greater propensities for depression and left untreated can increase one's risk for suicide (CDC, 2005).

Addressed in the proposed study is the need to explore adequately the phenomena of law enforcement suicide, by providing examples of appropriate coping strategies for officers dealing with difficult issues. Providing appropriate coping mechanisms may assist officers in recognizing the early signs and symptoms of depression, suicide, suicidal behavior, and mental illness. A qualitative phenomenological study is appropriate when addressing officer perceptions about the effect of training on the difficult issues of mental illness and officer suicide. By examining officer perceptions concerning the influence of training on dealing with difficult issues, themes may emerge to improve understand of the effects of training on law enforcement suicide.

More officers commit suicide each year in the United States than are killed in the line-of-duty (Kelly & Martin, 2006; Violanti, 2007). Officers who die in the line-of-duty are considered immortal heroes, while peers view officers who take their own lives as cowards (Violanti & Samuels, 2007). Depression alone does not indicate the susceptibility of attempted suicide. However, depression coupled with difficulties in diagnosing depression, self-medication and the lack of peer support during times of intense stress can increase one's susceptibility to suicide (Kelly & Martin, 2006; Waters & Ussery, 2007). Law enforcement training on difficult issues may inform officers and administration of the signs and symptoms of depression, the risks associated with suicide and suicidal behavior, and the fact that the number one killer of law enforcement personnel is suicide (Kelly & Martin, 2006).

Acknowledgement of law enforcement suicide as an epidemic is foundational to receiving adequate funding for training on officer suicide (Douglas, 1997; PSF, 2008b). Training may reduce stigmatization attached to issues of mental health, possibly helping to increase the number of officers seeking assistance for mental health issues (Perin, 2007). Training opens lines of communication between officers, supervisors, and command staff about difficult issues, reducing the number of officers believing their only option during difficult times is suicide. Training on difficult issues must be made available to every officer and must be proactive rather than reactive. Many law enforcement administrators take the mental health of law enforcement officers for granted (Kelley, 2005).

Due to the law enforcement culture, the actual number of officers who *eat their gun* every year is disguised (Hackett & Violanti, 2003). By disguising the actual number of officer suicides, departments not only lose officers to suicide, but also lose funding for training that could prevent the loss of life. The lack of concern shifts the focus away from officer suicide, allowing leadership time to rationalize the suicides as isolated incidents. The focus should not be on the misclassification, concealment, or rationalization of officer suicide, but rather on the fact suicide is preventable through awareness and training (Satcher, 1999; Violanti, 2007).

Law Enforcement Culture

Law enforcement culture significantly influences officer perceptions of incidents and officer expectations of trauma (Waters & Ussery, 2007). Extended exposure to traumatic events often results in intense psychological and emotional disorders (Gray & Lombardo, 2004). Waters and Ussery (2007) explained, "It is important to understand the predisposing factors, the nature of stressful events experienced by officers and . . . transient and long term response to these events" (p. 174). Officers learn to reduce and eliminate emotion, helping to insulate them from extremely stressful and traumatic events (Blum, 2000; Henry, 2004). However, the suppression and reduction of emotions leave officers more vulnerable to stress induced disorders (Weisinger, 1985). In the absence of psychological support from peers, officers are reluctant to discuss feelings about stressful and traumatic events. Such reluctance contributes to officers suffering silently from stress, depression, and substance abuse, all of which contribute to an increased risk of suicide (Cross & Ashley, 2004).

Culture is difficult to define due to the numerous definitions that exist (Hassell, 2006). Culture allows insiders to understand the behaviors, rituals, and structure of culture explicitly and outsiders to understand implicitly (Crank, 2004). According to Evans and Crank (2004):

> Culture is an enigma, a mysterious condensation of unity that prevails in all law enforcement agencies. You cannot see it, you cannot touch it, but you can feel it. No other occupation in the workforce in the United States is so shielded and enlivened by culture as is law enforcement. (p. 339)

Triandis (1994) defined culture in a primitive nature, in which groups of people develop coping mechanisms in order to communicate and survive. Subcultures are much more intimate, allowing individuals to develop much closer relationships. Within subcultures, occupational cultures exist. Individuals in occupational subcultures that experience increased levels of stress, traumatic incidents, and identifiable social roles often build trust and solidarity at faster rates than subcultures, which do not have similar experiences (Crank, 2004; Violanti, 2007).

Law enforcement is an occupation of extremes in which officers randomly patrol for extended periods of time and in mere seconds can be dispatched to events of life and death (Crank, 2004; Karlsson & Christianson 2003; Kelley, 2005). Occupations experiencing such extremes often find it necessary to reinforce shared beliefs within occupational boundaries (Brink, 2001; Stevens, 2005). The culture in which the law enforcement officer works is not always tangible and societal expectations are constantly changing, but the thought of taking a bullet for a fellow officer is a bond few individuals share. The dangers involved in police work often draw the individuals choosing law enforcement as career closer together, often closer than the traditional family unit (Crank, 2004; Quinn, 2005).

Individuals within law enforcement unit's exhibit shared values, beliefs, experiences and attitudes, ultimately defining the law enforcement family unit (Stevens, 2005). The average day of an officer consists of a range of calls to include dealing with "human misery, street-level combat situations, abused children, severe assaults, death, natural and human initiated disasters, and terrorism" (Violanti & Samuels, 2007, p. ix). Interactions with the public and other law enforcement personnel cause ideas, behaviors, and perceptions to become commonplace, and there are often shared beliefs among other officers. Law enforcement culture is founded on a Code of Silence (Crank, 2004; Quinn, 2005). The Code of Silence is a culmination of unwritten rules understood and protected from command staff to line officers (Quinn, 2005) and is common practice among most law enforcement agencies (Crank, 2004). A failure to adhere to the rules of the Code of Silence can cause an officer their job, risk negative labeling, face discipline, or face rejection from fellow officers (Quinn, 2005; Trautman, 2001).

The Code of Silence is an elusive shield, representing the uniform, the badge, the gun, and the power of law enforcement personnel (Frey, 2007). The Code of Silence is just as much a part of law enforcement as the gun and badge, acting as a protective mechanism of emotion and secrecy (Quinn, 2005). Emotions are to remain in check and are not to surface in front of others, especially fellow officers. The showing of emotion displays weakness in law enforcement culture (Baker, 1985; Blum, 2000). Open displays of emotion within law enforcement culture confirm the message that officers are not mentally or physically prepared for the battles they face (Crank, 2004).

The Code of Silence acts as mechanism for secretive behavior in which no one is to expose another officer or discuss unethical behavior, or misconduct. Officers cover each other no matter what the circumstance, or fear retaliation from peers. Cancino and Enriquez (2004) defined deviant behavior within law enforcement agencies as forms of social control by peers used to govern individual actions through forms of peer retaliation. Within the law enforcement culture, personal issues are put aside to protect to group as a whole. Carter (1985) defined the abuse and misuse of authority by officers as "an action . . . without regard to motive, intent, or malice that tends to injure, insult, tread on human dignity, manifest feelings of inferiority, and/or violate an inherent legal right of a member of the police constituency" (p. 322).

According to Reiner (1978), officers exhibit deviance internally towards the department or externally towards the community. Officers who do not comply with the Code of Silence are seen as deviant, rather than the classified deviant behavior, for which the Code of Silence is used to disguise. The Code of Silence is an unwritten code about what is and is not acceptable within police circles (Cancino & Enriquez, 2004). Law enforcement culture provides officers the ability to abuse power, through corruptive acts. The abuse of power and corruption are behaviors that are prevalent in law enforcement today (Crank, 2004). Deviance and dysfunction are so commonplace that such behavior is a major focus in law enforcement academy (Kelley, 2005). According to Reiner (1978), the element of power and force associated with police work often attracts men who seek such authority. The Code of Silence perpetuates misconduct and deviant behavior because it guarantees secrecy to all members (Blum, 2000; Quinn, 2005).

Officers exhibit a bond through the commonality of the badge (Crank, 2004). The badge is symbolic to the lawful power granted to law enforcement officials and a personal indicator of winning every fight. The badge symbolizes an expectation of control in which the officer is expected to maintain control, whether real or perceived (Blum, 2000). The mindset of any officer is survival at all costs, believing everyone on the shift is going home (Quinn, 2005). The survival mindset becomes second nature in the minds and bodies of all law enforcement recruits.

The Code of Silence prevails through communication and the sharing of stories (Quinn, 2005). Information sharing is crucial to officer survival and foundational to law enforcement culture. The sharing of information during shift-change comes in the form of stories, jokes, and cynical comments about public and departmental interactions. Officers become cynical over the ways of the world and about the justice system, they hope to change (Niederhoffer, 1967). The Code of Silence is a protective mechanism for all officers, but even within the individual department, divides exist between line officers and command staff; there is an us versus them mentality.

Law enforcement is a form of social control and a system of authority reacting and responding to deviant types of behavior (Black, 1980). The encounter between law enforcement officers and citizens has many dimensions in social space and each of the distinct relationships helps explain how and why law enforcement reacts with the community. Law enforcement officials use social control to gain compliance and resolution to numerous situations. Citizens develop measures of self-help in order to avoid involving law enforcement (Black, 1980). According to Ross (2000), law enforcement and the public maintain legitimacy by maintaining a legal role in the relationship. Departmental liability depends largely on the conduct of the individual officer, insofar that the conduct of the individual officer or an act by such an officer does not impede the rights' of others (Worrall, 2001). Officer support of the Code of Silence allows the subculture to maintain secrecy, maladaptive coping mechanisms, and deviant behavior (Kappeler, Sluder, & Alpert, 1998). Durkheim classified the absence of morality when concerning individual rights' as *anomie*.

Niederhoffer (1967) categorized anomie by a lack of concern for others, which leads to uncertainty, disappointment, estrangement, and desolation. Anomie is relatively absent within law enforcement culture using the Code of Silence to produce solidarity among officers. Niederhoffer (1967) explained law enforcement officers should be "tied to the law, but because they learn to manipulate it, the law can become nothing but a means to an end" (p. 97). While officers uphold the law, over the course of their careers they learn how to manipulate people and circumstances. According to Niederhoffer (1967), deviant behavior was promoted by the Code of Silence, as reflected in the following excerpt:

> The license to disregard the law in order to enforce it . . . may kill where necessary . . . may destroy property and invade privacy; . . . may make arrest merely on the grounds of suspicion; . . . may disregard traffic regulations. The sense of power often corrupts him into a belief that he is superior to the law. (p. 97)

Officers often believe they are indestructible and above refute, which contributes to increased levels of secrecy and cynicism (Crank, 2004; Tuck, 2009). The cynical officer "finds it easier to reduce commitment to the social system and its values"

(Niederhoffer, 1967, p. 101). The ability to reduce commitment of law enforcement culture, coupled with increased cynicism, contributes to officer isolation, which may "lead to psychological anomie and even suicide" (Niederhoffer, 1967, p. 101).

Law Enforcement Suicide

Law enforcement officials witness many tragic events over the course of their careers, which can have long lasting effects on their emotional and physical well-being (Violanti, Castellano, O'Rourke, & Paton, 2006; Waters & Ussery, 2007). According to the PSF (2008b), of the 18,000 law enforcement agencies nationwide, less than 2% offered any type of suicide training (para. 2). More officers commit suicide each year in the United States than are killed in the line-of-duty (Kelly & Martin, 2006). Peers classify officers who die in the in-the-of-duty as immortal heroes, while they view officers who take their own lives as cowards or weak (Perin, 2007). Depression alone does not indicate the susceptibility to attempted suicide; however, one's susceptibility increases when depression is combined with difficulties in diagnosing depression, self-medication, and lack of peer support during times of intense stress (Kelly & Martin, 2006; Waters & Ussery, 2007).

Cultural norms engrossed by law enforcement include privacy, secrecy, and shame, all of which influence the decision to come forward for help (Crank, 2004). Law enforcement culture and leadership dictate behaviors and actions of all officers, from the rookie to the veteran, and suicide is common across all ranks. Vigilant and proactive leadership assists in breaking through barriers formed around law enforcement culture. Administrators must take a proactive approach, which includes acknowledging that suicide is the number one killer of law enforcement officers. Training on difficult issues may help reduce stigma attached to mental illness and may allow officers to seek assistance with issues of mental health.

Methods of suicide vary depending on organizational culture. For example, law enforcement officers are more prone to commit suicide with their duty weapon (Violanti, 2007). The duty weapon is an extension of the officer. A majority of officer suicides involve gunshot wounds to the head and upper extremities (Violanti, 2007). Officers' knowledge of the firearm and the deadly consequences of firearm injuries minimize officer survival (Violanti, 2007).

Nagourney (2007) explained 90% of suicide attempts with a firearm are successful, or completed suicides (para. 6). The high numbers of successful suicide attempts are due in part to the lethal component of the firearm and the proximity of the firearm to the body. The lethal component of the firearm, coupled with placement of the firearm to the upper extremities and training in the use of the firearm by law enforcement officers, increases the lethal component of the suicide attempt (Violanti, 2007). Reducing opportunity for the chosen method of suicide, the duty weapon, does not mean officers will choose an alternative method of suicide (Violanti, 2007). Rather, the displacement of the chosen method may prevent suicide (Fendrich, Kryesi, Grossman, Wislar, & Freeman, 1998; Violanti, 2007). The duty weapon is a symbolic extension of the officer; "it is a symbol of their authority, identity as guardians of the law, and mastery over the environment. The value of the firearm becomes obvious when it is taken away" (Violanti, 2007, p. 65).

Socialization practices predispose law enforcement officers to suicide and suicidal behavior (Violanti, 2007). Officers may fear negative labels, losing employment, losing individual identity, and peer retaliation if they discuss the issue of officer suicide. Law enforcement culture perpetuates issues of shame and secrecy, making it more difficult for officers to ask for assistance during difficult times. Many times, more importance exists in the physical well-being of the officer, rather than the psychological well-being (Violanti & Samuels, 2007). If an officer commits suicide, shame and anger fill the department placing undue stress on the department, fellow officers, and family members who believe something could have been done to prevent the tragedy.

Administrators do not talk about the deceased individual in an attempt to ignore the suicide and to avoid the possibility of copycat suicides (Violanti & Hackett, 2007). Officers who kill themselves become the cowards who could not handle the responsibility handed to them (Violanti, 2007). The department and the badge are tarnished and it appears nothing can change the scenario. Within the law enforcement culture, officers are conditioned to prove themselves to the department and more importantly to their fellow officers (Crank, 2004; Harrison, 1998; Hassell, 2006). Asking for assistance, whether to administrators or fellow officers about issues of mental illness, can lead to an officer being placed on desk duty, the loss of the duty weapon, or even the loss of a job. The consequences are what many officers fear when asking for assistance and fear may further perpetuate mixed feelings about seeking assistance (Burke & Mikkelsen, 2007).

Risk Factors of Law Enforcement Suicide

Law enforcement officers, firefighters, and emergency medical workers have higher than average suicide rates (Pegula, 2004). The characteristics and risk factors of suicide among law enforcement personnel include exposure to occupational hazards; availability of firearms; alcohol consumption, drug use, and drug abuse; high levels of stress; PTSD; financial problems; and relationship issues (PSF, 2008b; Rudofossi, 2007).

Officers declared successful in dealing with high levels of stress are often successful

because of their ability to develop creative stress reducing strategies, which effectively

deal with and reduce surmounting and continuous stress (Waters & Ussery, 2007).

According to Aamodt and Stalnaker (2006), the profile of the law enforcement

officer, deputy sheriff, or corrections officer who commits suicide is a 36 year old, White

male, with approximately 12 years of law enforcement service. He typically commits

suicide when off-duty, at home, using a duty weapon to head. He is typically facing

relationship issues (p. 387). In addition, the individual typically has low or declining on-

duty evaluations and demonstrated reckless behavior (PSF, 2008a).

According to the PSF (2008b), law enforcement officers take their own lives at a

rate of one every 17 hours, accounting for approximately 450 officer's suicide deaths per

year. Law enforcement suicides from 2004-2008 averaged 429 (see Table 1, p. 3).

Douglas (1997) explained the number of law enforcement suicides could be as high as

500 per year in the United States (p. 22). Law enforcement suicides are often concealed

or misclassified due to issues of insurance and shame (Kelly & Martin, 2006; Violanti,

2007; WHO, 2000). The concealment of law enforcement suicide makes accurate

reporting nearly impossible, causing a lack of governmental funding for agencies

experiencing officer suicide and agencies needing PSA training (PSF, 2008b). The

psychological trauma of 9/11 lead to increased numbers of emergency service workers

committing suicide. The events of 9/11 had significant effects on the mental health of

many who were involved and who watched the trauma through forms of media (Violanti

et al., 2006). During this time, suicide deaths of emergency service workers were still high in comparison to other occupations (CDC, 2005; Violanti, Castellano, O'Rourke, & Paton, 2006).

In 1997, the PSF (2008a) conducted a nationwide study about the possible reasons law enforcement officers commit suicide. The study included nine law enforcement agencies with a 98% response rate from 500 officers about reasons why officers commit suicide (PSF, 2008a). According to the results, officers may take their own lives for the following reasons: death of a spouse or child, terminal illness, killing someone in anger, isolation, sexual accusations, arrests or indictment, job loss, conviction of a crime, and jail or imprisonment (PSF, 2008a).

Suicide applies to all deaths, which result in death of the victim, whether the act of suicide was considered a positive or negative act (Durkheim, 1979). Suicide is a deeply rooted crisis in society (Durkheim, 1979; Violanti, 2007). Freud (1935) deemed suicide an individual expression of hostility and self-destruction. Individuals suffering from mental illness often exhibit the signs and symptoms of suicidal behavior. Many of the individuals only want to stop the pain (Violanti, 1995).

Law enforcement is a demanding career, placing a great deal of stress on the men and women in uniform (Burke & Mikkelsen, 2007; Waters & Ussery, 2007). Law enforcement is a non-stop job in which tragedy is witnessed day-after-day (Crank, 2004). The deterioration of the body is tragic, but the decline of the psyche and emotional well-being of officers takes an even greater toll (Tuck, 2009). Law enforcement is a stressful occupation, but without proper communication and training, stress builds, leaving lasting scars on the psyche of officers (Tuck, 2009). The risk of suicide increases within occupational subcultures, such as law enforcement, where there are high levels of stress, trauma, and identifiable social roles (Cross & Ashley, 2004). Law enforcement officers are seven times more likely to commit suicide than the general population (Tate, 2004). Law enforcement is a stressful occupation built on a culmination of acute life stressors (Liberman et al., 2002; Waters & Ussery, 2007). Prolonged exposure to stress or stressful events contributes to declining mental function (Heim et al., 2009). Unaddressed mental health issues can lead to depression, mental illness, a breakdown in appropriate occupational boundaries, increased sick time, decreased morale and productivity, suicide, and homicide (Cross & Ashley, 2004; Waters & Ussery, 2007). Depression may contribute to physical illness, accidents, and a lack of group cohesion (Kelley, 2005).

Law enforcement burnout warning signs.

According to Maslach and Jackson (1986), burnout was a syndrome in which individuals in service type jobs had a greater propensity for mental exhaustion, due to attitudes and depersonalization. Law enforcement is a stressful occupation (He, Zhao, & Archbold, 2002; Kroes, 1976). Increased levels of stress have been associated with a "high incidence of physical ailments and psychological problems that affect work performance" (Morash, Haarr, & Kwak, 2006, p. 26). Overexposure to stress can cause burnout, decreased personal drive, and an abandonment of law enforcement work (Maslach, 1976; Violanti & Aron, 1994).

Law enforcement burnout manifests in three definitive ways: physical burnout, occupational burnout, and family burnout (PSF, 2008a). Physical signs of officer burnout include fatigue, illness, or injury; muscle strain; physiological symptoms of depression and anxiety; sleeping problems; and pressure behind the sternum (PSF, 2008a).

Occupational signs of officer burnout include increased negative contacts with the public, isolation and low morale, loss of productivity, increased alcohol consumption, increased absenteeism, increased risk taking, vehicle accidents, and over *personalizing* the job (PSF, 2008a). Signs of family burnout include strain on family members (Loo, 2004), relationship issues, lack of communication, self-medication with drugs and alcohol, marital problems (Waters & Ussery, 2007), family conflict, and domestic violence (Waters & Ussery, 2007).

Stress and post-traumatic stress on law enforcement.

Law enforcement officers embark on a career in which optimal physical health is not only essential, but can be the difference between life and death (Kelley, 2005). Surmounting stress causes many officers to end up in early retirement due to stress disorders, placing the officer's emotional well-being in question (Jaramillo, et al., 2005; Waters & Ussery, 2007). Masculinity is stressed in law enforcement; officers are expected to be tough and self-sufficient. The suppression of emotions resulting from traumatic and stressful events increases the chance for stress-induced illnesses (Waters & Ussery, 2007). Stress is a major contributor to depression, especially when an accumulation of stress is placed on the individual (Janata, 2008; Klein & Wender, 2005). In an attempt to return the body to a normal functioning state, the body secretes hormones during times of increased and sustained stress. A majority of law enforcement stress occurs while on patrol, within the officer's agency, and within the officer's residence (PSF, 2008).

Long-standing and reoccurring stress leaves the body depleted of hormones necessary for normal body function (Janata, 2008). Van Praag (2004) explained stress was brought on by a multitude of emotions including: dishonor, remorse, bitterness, maliciousness, hopelessness, and helplessness. Each emotion surfaces in varying degrees and combinations. Subsequent perceptions of emotions "are equally diverse and range from thoughts of revenge, of homicide and suicide, of rebelliousness or resignation, of willful attempts to forget, suppress or to transform the adversity into a meaningful experience" (van Praag, 2004, p. 80). Suicide contemplation and ideation increase stress, in turn reducing an individual's ability to cope, resulting in depression or maladaptive coping mechanisms (Joiner, 2005; van Praag, 2004).

The lack of early intervention in diagnosing depression can lead to a severe form of depression known as clinical depression (Kelly & Martin, 2006; USPHS, 1999). According to Diamond (2003), clinical depression results from altered brain chemicals. A misunderstanding of chemical imbalances in the brain leads many to label individuals suffering from such imbalances as weak. Chemical imbalances can happen to anyone at any time and can occur due to a multitude of reasons (Waters & Ussery, 2007). Self-medication is often the result of individuals trying to end the pain associated with depression. Self-medication also contributes to the concealment of the signs and symptoms of depression (Andrew, 2008).

Officers suffering from depression may also suffer from PTSD, another warning sign of suicide. Post-traumatic stress disorder is an anxiety disorder resulting from the body's normal response to an abnormal circumstance, in which daily functioning, such as sleep, relationships, and work are disrupted (Kates, 1999; PSF, 2008). Post-traumatic stress disorder is often the result of a debilitating, life-threatening event (PSF, 2008). A majority of officers experience PTSD at some point during their career (Mullins, 2001).

Former director of the New York Police Counseling Services and retired Lieutenant James F. Devine stated, "PTSD is a greater cop killer than all the guns ever fired at police officers" (Kates, 2008, p. 1).

Many argue that initial hiring procedures assist in alleviating incidents of mental illness in law enforcement ranks (Kelley, 2005). Law enforcement officers are required to pass several psychological screenings prior to gaining employment (Mullins, 2001). Law enforcement officers appear to be more stable and better attuned to the stresses they encounter, and better able to adapt and overcome a culmination of unique situations. Officers are hired being of sound body and mind, so "there must be something about the job of policing that causes a psychological change and leads to a heightened state of suicide" (Mullins, 2001, p. 258). According to Kelley (2005), law enforcement administrators take for granted the mental health of law enforcement recruits, "as something achieved independently through genetics, socialization, and personal experience" (p. 7). Individuals within the career fields of disaster relief, law enforcement, and firefighting are more prone to witnessing critical incidents, resulting in PTSD. The possibility of completed suicide increases in individuals with PTSD (Hackett & Violanti, 2003).

Limited Research

Current literature on suicide and suicide theory is limited, because theorists such as Freud and Durkheim are considered foundational in the understanding of suicide and suicide theory, and though there is much debate and speculation about their works, there have not been any major contributions to the field of suicide theory in over 50 years. The unique nature of suicide and the groups who commit suicide often witness suicide as a distinct way to define further the subgroup. Culture often influences individual method and reason behind suicide (Burke & Mikkelsen, 2007). Reducing available methods of suicide (e.g., guns, knives, pills, ropes), may reduce the number of completed suicides Fendrich et al. (1998) suggested merely eliminating initial methods of suicide (e.g., guns, knives, pills, ropes) that many individuals will not choose alternative methods. Culture often dictates the method of suicide and law enforcement officials are associated with guns. According to Marcus (1996), "Nine out of ten officers who commit suicide do so using their own guns" (p. 21). The elimination of a weapon in the hand of a suicidal individual may postpone the act temporarily or altogether (Violanti, 2007).

Suicide is often an impulsive act resulting from an accumulation of incidents or outcomes (Jamison, 1999). Though suicide is often an impulsive act, time and energy are involved in the planning stages (Jamison, 1999). If closely addressed, many warning signs of impending suicide exist (Hackett & Violanti, 2003). The impulsive act of officer suicide, coupled with firearms availability and officer knowledge about the use of the firearm, allows minimal time for officers to reconsider their actions.

The use of keywords [behavioral theory, cognitive theory, law enforcement culture, law enforcement stressors, law enforcement suicide, mental illness, and suicide] helped to retrieve 2000 articles from specific databases available in the University of Phoenix Apollo Library. No set standardized system exists for measuring the size of a digital library; each institutional library has different sets of focus, based on the programs offered. Besides availability of primary literature resources, the library also houses secondary databases from other institutions. Examples of housed databases included in the search were the ProQuest Database, EBSCOhost, Emerald, InfoTrac OneFile,

Journals@Ovid, PsychARTICLES, and Questia. Review of abstracts of articles retrieved by key word resulted in the elimination of 1400 articles, whose abstract content did not fit the criteria for inclusion into this literature review. In-depth content review of the remaining 600 resulted in the elimination of all but 192 articles retained for relevance, fit, and substantive value to this literature review.

Although only 65 of the 192 were recent articles within the last 5 years, the 126 articles older than 5 years were a strong fit and of significant substantive value to this literature review. The total number of all 65 recent articles exceeds the 50 article minimum requirement for a doctoral dissertation review. Furthermore, failure to include the 126 articles older than 5 years in this review leaves this literature review incomplete, incoherent, and imbalanced. The critical nature of the 126 articles demanded inclusion to provide explanatory coherence of theories examined in the review. The caveat in the inclusion of the 126 articles was the violation of School of Advanced Studies recent article rule, which demands that at least more than 85% of articles included in literature review must be no more than 5 years old. Rigid application of the rule would have resulted in an incoherent review of the literature.

Conclusion

Suicide is a public health concern of epidemic proportions (Satcher, 1999). Suicide is exacerbated in subcultures experiencing high levels of stress, trauma, and identifiable social roles, such as in law enforcement (Cross & Ashley, 2004; Violanti, 2007). More officers commit suicide than are killed in the line-of-duty (Tate, 2004).

The nature of law enforcement contributes to the accumulation of officer stress. Prolonged exposure to stress and trauma contribute to declining mental health (Heim et al., 2009), in-turn, leading to maladaptive coping mechanisms such as increased alcohol use, to deal with the inter pain and turmoil. The use of maladaptive coping mechanisms increases peer isolation and increases the chances of overlooking the signs and symptoms of depression.

Suicide theories exist in an attempt to classify and explain suicide (Freud, 1935). Suicide theories often try to explain reasons for suicide, but more importantly, theory does not reduce the number of law enforcement suicides. Training may increase sensitivity of mental health issues, while decreasing the stigmatization attached to mental health issues. Stigmatization of individuals suffering from mental illness is the number one reason why so many suffer in silence (DMH, 2006). Reducing stigmatization of mental illness may allow individuals who suffer to seek assistance sooner.

Training, behavior modification, and knowledge contribute to stigma reduction (USPHS, n.d.). Stigma perpetuates individual and group level value systems through the media and the law (Sales & Kahle, 1980). Law enforcement officers, through the nature of their work, encounter individuals suffering from mental illness. Law enforcement officers' contact with the mentally ill, coupled with a lack of training on difficult issues, leaves officers labeling individuals suffering from mental illness as problematic. Officers suffering from mental illness often suffer in silence because they fear retaliation from peers, or the possibility of losing jobs and identities. Law enforcement to an officer is not a job, but rather a way of life (Crank, 2004). The thought of taking away one's livelihood can seem like a death sentence.

A gap of current literature exists on the topic of law enforcement suicide. A lack of literature exists that links law enforcement culture and the idea behind the Code of

Silence. Members of the law enforcement community view officer suicide as shameful, causing many officer suicides to be misclassified or concealed (Violanti, 2007). In a final attempt to protect the family of the deceased officer, the deceased officers employing agency often classify the death accidental, allowing the family to collect insurance.

Law enforcement suicide is secret many in the law enforcement community would rather not discuss (Violanti, 2008). Many do not discuss the topic because the lack of literature on the topic shows a problem does not exist (Violanti, 2007). Officers resort to the Code of Silence, as a means of silencing concerns from outsiders about the high number of yearly officer suicides (Violanti et al., 2006). Officers are protected by the Code of Silence and inadvertently are expected to remain silent about the topic of officer suicide (Kelley, 2005).

Summary

Chapter 2 contains the literature review of the theory of suicide and a chronological characterization of the research associated with law enforcement suicide. Chapter 2 includes an examination of the relevant literature concerning suicide theory, cognitive and behavioral learning theory, and stigmas associated with officer suicide. Characterizations exist about law enforcement culture and how culture may perpetuate the issue of officer suicide. A primary objective of the proposed qualitative phenomenological study is to uncover officer perceptions about training's impact on officer suicide.

Chapter 3 begins with information concerning the research method and design appropriateness. Included in chapter 3 is a discussion of the study population and sample, informed consent and confidentiality, and data collection procedures. Chapter 3 includes information concerning instrument validity. Chapter 3 concludes with a discussion of data analysis techniques deemed appropriate for the study.

Chapter 3: Method

The purpose of the study was to explore the lived experiences of law enforcement officers concerning perceptions of care by administrators and peers and the influence of mental health training on the incidence of officer suicide. Uncovering perceptions about the role of mental health training among law enforcement officers may facilitate the development of an effective training program that may positively affect officer perceptions on the phenomenon of suicide among law enforcement officers. A lack of acknowledgement by law enforcement administrators about officer suicide suggests a lack of importance about the topic. Suicide is the leading cause of law enforcement officer deaths nationwide (Violanti, 2007). More officers die from suicide than are killed in the line-of-duty (Violanti, 2007). A lack of acknowledgement by administration about issues killing law enforcement officers reinforces the message to officers they are supposed to solve problems, not create problems (Kirschman, 2007).

Approximately 1 million individuals commit suicide annually worldwide (WHO, 2006), with approximately 30 thousand suicides occurring in the United States (CDC, 2005; Jamison, 1999). Shared value systems within subcultures, such as law enforcement, where suicide is viewed as taboo compounds the frequency of suicide. Law enforcement officers are seven times more likely to commit suicide than the general population (Tate, 2004). Violanti (2007) suggested law enforcement suicide rates increased due to a lack of officer training on difficult situations such as police suicide. Among the 18,000 police departments nationwide, less than 2%, or 360 departments, provide any type of suicide training or education (PSF, 2008b).

Chapter 3 begins with a discussion of the research method and design appropriateness. Chapter 3 includes information regarding the study population, sample, and the informed consent process. Chapter 3 includes a discussion of the instrumentation and the data collection and analysis process. Chapter 3 concludes with a summary of key points and a transition to chapter 4.

Appropriateness of Research Method

The purpose of the study was to explore the lived experiences of law enforcement officers concerning perceptions of care by administrators and peers and the influence of mental health training on the incidence of officer suicide. Moustakas (1994) explained a qualitative method "provides a logical, systematic, and coherent resource for carrying out the analysis and synthesis needed to arrive at essential descriptions of experience" (p. 47). The qualitative method was appropriate when research variables are unclear and inadequate amounts of literature exist (Neuman, 2005; Strauss & Corbin, 1990). The personal experience provides meaningful data because the data will be individually unique (Kirk & Miller, 1986; Maxfield & Babbie, 2005; Moustakas, 1994; Neuman, 2005), and some degree of truth exists within the data of qualitative studies (Silverman, 2004; Strauss & Corbin, 1990).

A lack of literature and quantifiable types of data contribute to the choice of a qualitative method. The focus of qualitative methodology is on personal meanings and individual experiences (Neuman, 2005), such as the meanings and experiences associated with officer suicide by law enforcement officers. Officers described perceptions of their lived experiences regarding the impact training has on reducing the number of yearly officer suicides. Perceptions, though subjective and biased, provide insight into the phenomenon of officer suicide. Even well intentioned researchers must remain cognizant of the prejudices and preconceived notions they possess (Neuman, 2005).

When research variables are unknown, in-depth interviews with fewer participants are common in qualitative research (Strauss & Corbin, 1990). Individuals commit suicide for a number of reasons. The reasons why law enforcement officers kill themselves can be perplexing. The complex nature of suicide includes numerous variables and motives may remain unknown. The unique nature of suicide is further complicated within occupations such as law enforcement, which are defined by increased levels of stress, trauma, and identifiable social roles; suicide risks increase within these types of organizations (Cross & Ashley, 2004).

Quantitative research is concerned with measurement, techniques, and design issues, because planning and analysis happen prior to data collection (Neuman, 2005). Quantitative research does not provide the richness of a qualitative design. A mixed method approach is feasible, but also limits the overall insight into the phenomena of law enforcement suicide.

Appropriateness of Design

A quantitative design was not appropriate because the use of the design would not provide the in-depth interpretation of the lived experience. Researchers using quantitative designs do not allow for the open communication of the event being researched by the study participant. A phenomenological design was appropriate for the research study because with a phenomenological approach participant perceptions could be used to challenge common beliefs and misconceptions about the phenomenon being researched (Kirk & Miller, 1986; Moustakas, 1994). The use of a phenomenological research design allows for the extraction of individual perceptions, producing a more meaningful explanation of common daily experiences (van Manen, 1990). Phenomenology attempts to seek personal truth and limits of personal truth (Sokolowski, 2007). The use of a phenomenological approach allows researchers to gather information and knowledge about participants' perceptions of the impact training had on the incidence of law enforcement suicide. A phenomenological method was appropriate for the study because phenomenology is a study of the lived human experience (Moustakas, 1994).

Moustakas (1994) explained that the use of a phenomenological design placed the focus on individual perception. Phenomenology is a major "source of knowledge, the source that cannot be doubted" (Moustakas, 1994, p. 52). Phenomenology consists of a more meaningful understanding of experiences without the possibility of efficient theory, but builds clarification of the deeper understanding gained (van Manen, 1990). Moustakas (1994) explained phenomenological research originated from a first-person account of personal experiences.

A foundation of understanding exists within subcultures, allowing outside cultures to understand better subcultures. In the study, individual perceptions rather than group perceptions are addressed. Ethnographic studies involve broad formal and informal interviews that "may be pursued in a variety of social settings that allow for direct observations of the activities of the group being studied" (Moustakas, 1994, p. 1). Emphasis in ethnographic studies is on group interactions through observation, whereas emphasis in a phenomenological research design is on individual perception, senses, and experiences (Moustakas, 1994).

Strauss and Corbin (1990) explained grounded theory as a theoretical explanation of the themes within the data. Grounded theory has a lower rate of applicability to motivations for such human behavior and cannot successfully explain human motivations on a larger scale (Strauss & Corbin (1990). Grounded theory was not appropriate for the current study because grounded theory lacks the wide applicability of understanding, the motives behind law enforcement suicide, and lacks the ability to make broad connections between training's influence and the high number of yearly law enforcement suicides. Grounded theory allows a researcher to modify an existing theory and works from an inductive approach, moving from specific to general (Glaser & Strauss, 1999; Strauss & Corbin, 1990).

The purpose of the study was to explore the lived experiences of law enforcement officers concerning perceptions of care by administrators and peers and the influence of mental health training on the incidence of officer suicide. Case studies focus more on identifying and describing group-type activities, rather than the behaviors of the (Yin, 2009). The phenomenon of law enforcement suicide is explained in the individual context of law enforcement and in terms of a subculture, displaying behavioral patterns of a larger group or context. The focus of case studies is on specific events, individuals, and activities, at more in-depth levels, but also includes a set of specific boundaries of time and space (Neuman, 2005).

Research Questions

Exploration of the phenomenon of law enforcement suicide was directed by the following research question: *What are the lived experiences and perceptions of law enforcement officers concerning the effect the Police Suicide Awareness (PSA) training on the incidence of suicide among law enforcement officers?* The interview questions for the study were in an open-ended context, so participants could provide in-depth answers. By using open-ended questions, the in-depth answers provided allowed for the identification of common themes about the phenomenon researched.

Population

According to Albright, personal assistant to the Executive Director of the Illinois Law Enforcement Training and Standards Board, Madison and Saint Clair Counties, Illinois have 43 municipal agencies, 2 county agencies, and 1 state agency (S. Albright, personal communication, June 01, 2009). The population selected from Saint Louis County, Missouri included only federal law enforcement officers. The target population includes only sworn law enforcement officers. The target population includes White, male officers with a minimum of 5 years of law enforcement experience. The study population included law enforcement officers from Madison and Saint Clair Counties in Illinois, and Saint Louis County, Missouri, because the geographic region contained municipal, county, state, and federal law enforcement agencies. The geographic region of Madison County contains 515 full-time officers and 38 part-time officers, totaling 553 officers (J. Fulton, personal communication, June 15, 2009). The geographic location of Saint Clair County contains 602 full-time officers and 1061 part-time officers (J. Fulton, personal communication, June 15, 2009). Saint Louis County, Missouri consists of municipal, 1 county, 1 state, and federal law enforcement agencies. Officers working within Saint Louis County, Missouri, participated using snowballing and did not want the type of agency they were employed with to be identified, as they feared that their administrators would identify them.

According to the CDC (2005), White males were at a much greater-risk for completed suicide. Law enforcement is a male dominated occupation, where males account for over 90 % of all police personnel (Polisar & Milgram, 1998). The increased risk of suicide within the law enforcement population may exist due to the increased representation of males in law enforcement and males in general, accounting for the highest number of completed suicides nationwide (CDC, 2005; NCHS, 2005).

Informed Consent

Harm is minimized when all participants receive moral and ethical consideration (Barnett, Johnson-Greene, Wise, & Bucky, 2007). All participants received moral and ethical consideration by obtaining the informed consent prior to participation in the study. Informed consent includes providing potential participants with enough information to "weigh the potential benefits and risks of both participation and lack of participation" (Barnett et al., 2007, p. 80). Participants were at least 18 years of age and deemed mentally competent.

All participants were required to provide voluntary consent. Participants read, signed, and returned an informed consent form (see Appendix B) before consideration for the study. Informed consent was acquired using Neuman's (2005) statements regarding informed consent. Participants were advised of any risks or harm them might be subjected to, but harm and risk were minimized (Neuman, 2005). All participants remain anonymous, and collected data and interview paperwork will be kept confidential (Neuman, 2005). Participants were made aware of their right to receive information regarding the study (Neuman, 2005).

Participation in the study was voluntary. Voluntary included the ability for participants to terminate participation at any time and for any reason, without consequence. Participants withdrawing from the study were informed that they could do so in writing, by phone, or in person. Participants did not receive compensation for participation in the study. No participants withdrew from the study. Participants received a summary of the research findings. Participants were identified using alphanumeric codes. Participant information, data, and research will remain confidential and will be kept in a locked vault only accessible to the researcher. The confidential information is password protected and stored for 3 years. Upon completion of the 3-year time requirement, all documentation will be shredded and the hard drive erased of all study information. Participants were informed verbally and in writing about data collection procedures and the procedures in place to destroy study information after completion of the study.

Sampling Frame

The purpose of the study was to explore the lived experiences of law enforcement officers concerning perceptions of care by administrators and peers and the influence of mental health training on the incidence of officer suicide. The sampling technique was purposeful and "rich" (Patton, 1990, p. 169). Purposeful sampling helps to develop a deeper understanding of a smaller population, rather than generalize to a larger population (Neuman, 2005), and involves the intentional selection of participants from a specific population in which one wants to understand some type of phenomenon (Moustakas, 1994). Purposeful sampling provides rich data, which may provide a deeper understanding of the phenomenon (Patton, 1990). The sample size is not generalizable to a larger population, but the small sample size allowed for a richer, more meaningful understanding and interpretation of officer perceptions about the phenomenon being researched (Moustakas, 1994; Patton, 1990)

The objective of qualitative research was not to generalize results from a sample to a specific population. Rather, the objective was to build an in-depth understanding of the phenomenon being researched (Neuman, 2005). Using a purposive sampling technique ensured participants emulated the at-risk population for suicide. The use of purposeful sampling provided a deeper understanding of the phenomenon (Neuman, 2005).

Sampling

To be included in the study, participants must: (a) be White, (b) male law enforcement officers, (c) have a minimum of 5 years law enforcement service, (d) work in departments with at least 10 full-time officers, and (e) work within Madison or Saint Clair Counties, Illinois, and Saint Louis County, Missouri. These three counties were appropriate choices due to the close proximity of the agencies to each other and the belief that face-to-face interviews enhance the study of the phenomenon. Municipal, county, and federal law enforcement agencies exist within all three counties.

Letters requesting inclusion in the study were sent to 12 municipal agencies and 2 county agencies in Madison and Saint Clair Counties, in Illinois. The officers participating from departments within Saint Louis County were identified using a snowballing technique. The officers who chose to participate did on their own behalf and were not required to receive approval from their employing agency. Appendix C contains a letter of inclusion from participating agencies. Eligible departments had a minimum of 10 full-time officers. Letters of inclusion were collected until 20 participants or data saturation occurred by departments showing an interest for inclusion in the study, this was based on the responses received. A point-of-contact from each department was needed and eligibility was determined by verbal confirmation from the point-of-contact.

By including three types of departments (i.e. municipal, county, and federal) in the interview process, the possibility of reaching data saturation across all law enforcement agencies is increased. Eligible department officers receive a 4-week response period to remain eligible. Department officials received notification of the eligibility status and possible dates and times for interviews. The permission to use premises form is located in Appendix D and only includes departments, which agreed to allow officers to participate and to use the officers department for the purpose of the interview.

The number of eligible participants from any single department is limited to four officers. A request was made for four randomly selected participants from each department. The first 20 officers identified from eligible departments were interviewed. If saturation is reached with the 20 selected participants, no additional interviews are conducted. If data saturation is not reached, interviews with participants continue until data saturation is reached.

Excluded from the study were females, non-law enforcement officers, non-White males, all officers with less than 5 years of police service, individuals outside the selected geographic region, and individuals within departments of less than 10 full-time officers. Due to the increased risk of suicide, White, male officers were selected (CDC, 2005). Groups not fulfilling the requirements of purposive sampling for the study are not included. White, male law enforcement officers were the selected population, as individuals outside of law enforcement would not contribute to the understanding of the phenomenon of law enforcement suicide. White, males account for the highest number of annual suicides in the United States, including those individuals in law enforcement, which is why the population was appropriate (CDC, 2005; Hackett & Violanti, 2003).

Because officers witness numerous traumatic events in a relatively short time, the officers are often considered established officers in fewer than 3 years on the force. The idea behind the study was to locate officers who are considered established and understand their roles in the department, within peer groups, and within the larger culture. Officers were chosen based on a match with the eligibility criteria. The eligibility criteria ensures a sample of seasoned officers who have gone through initial academy training and more than likely, have had additional training since the academy.

Interview participants were chosen using a purposeful sample of eligible law enforcement departments within Madison and Saint Clair Counties in Illinois, and Saint Louis County, Missouri. Once eligible departments were determined, individual officers from the departments were selected based on the study criteria. The point-of-contact person from each department provided a list of eligible participants willing to be included in the research study. Voluntary consent was required from all participants, even if departments choose to participate in the study. Interview participants were advised of the confidential and voluntary nature of the interview process. Interview participants were advised that they were under no obligation to participate in the interview process or the study. Participants deciding to withdrawal were able to do so in person, in writing, by phone, or email, whatever method was the most convenient and least invasive. No participants withdrew from the study. Immediate removal from the eligibility pool and the study occurred upon receipt of voluntary withdrawal. Individuals who chose to withdrawal were replaced as soon as possible. All participants were required to read and sign a consent form indicating the voluntary basis of their participation in the study. Participant confidentiality was maintained through an alphanumeric coding system.

Geographic Location

The population selected includes law enforcement officers from Madison and Saint Clair Counties in Illinois and Saint Louis County, Missouri. These counties were appropriate because they include municipal, county, and federal law enforcement agencies. Madison County, Illinois is located approximately 20 miles east of St. Louis, Missouri. Saint Clair County is located approximately 25 miles east of St. Louis, Missouri.

Instrumentation

Human science researchers possess many common traits and features (Moustakas, 1994). According to Moustakas (1994), the traits and features include the ability to distinguish qualitative from quantitative research approaches, while appreciating the value of the data produced by the qualitative method. For phenomenology to be beneficial, the focus must be on the totality of the experience, rather than segments of memory or specific occurrences of the participants. The purpose of the study was to find meaning within the experiences, rather than quantifiable types of measurement. The use of formal and informal interviews assisted in obtaining a first-hand account of the phenomenon of officer suicide. The data collected from the interview process was vital to the comprehension of the human experience. Officer perceptions may help explain what, if any, impact training had on developing the necessary skills to deal with difficult personal issues. Interview questions were derived from the literature review concerning the reasons why law enforcement officers are killing themselves at a rate of seven times the general population (Tate, 2004). Behaviors and experiences assimilate, forming a relationship that looks at both the pieces of the entire perception.

Interview questions were worded to gain an understanding of the participants' perceptions, while trying to view the experience with new eyes from the phenomenological viewpoint (van Manen, 1990). A researcher must disregard preconceived notions, prejudices, stigma, and perceptions about the reasons why law enforcement officers kill themselves (Moustakas, 1994). The transcendental phenomenological approach is the ability to remain neutral and receptive to the experience (Moustakas, 1994).

The perceptions of law enforcement officers about the effects of mental health training on the incidence of officer suicide will be addressed with 7 demographic questions and 18 interview questions. The interview questions are broad, allowing participants to expound the presented questions. Demographic questions included:

1. What is your gender?

2. What is your race?

3. What is your age?

4. Are you a sworn or commissioned full-time law enforcement officer within Madison or Saint Clair Counties, Illinois, or Saint Louis County, Missouri?

5. What type of law enforcement agency are you employed with?

6.   What title (i.e., trooper, sheriff's deputy, police officer) do you hold with your employing agency?

7.   How many years have you been a sworn or commissioned law enforcement officer?

The following questions were interview questions. Officer perception of care and impact of training on officer suicide were the focus of the interview questions.

1.   What are some of the most difficult situations you have encountered in your law enforcement career?

2.   Based on your experience with your present law enforcement agency, what types of training have you received regarding difficult law enforcement issues?

3.   Based on your experience with your present law enforcement agency, how do you believe the provided training was useful?

4.   Thinking back on the training you received, what could have been improved to increase the effectiveness of the training?

5.   Based on your experience with your present law enforcement agency, in what ways do your peers show concern about your overall well-being?

6.   Based on your experience with your present law enforcement agency, in what ways does administration show concern about your overall well-being?

7.   Based on your experience with your present law enforcement agency, how does the concern provided by administrators differ from the concern provided by peers?

8. Based on your experience with your present law enforcement agency, what have you learned through training concerning the signs and symptoms of stress and depression?

9. In your opinion or experience, what is the effect of training, if any, on stress and depression in officers?

10. What attempts do you make to minimize stress and depression in yourself?

11. What attempts do your peers make to minimize stress and depression in fellow officers?

12. Based on your experience with your present law enforcement agency, in what ways do administrators strive to minimize officer stress and depression?

13. How do you feel that law enforcement contributes to stress and depression in officers?

14. How do you see the Culture hindering officers seeking assistance for issues concerning stress and depression?

15. How do you see the Culture influencing the acknowledgement of officer stress and depression?

16. Based on your experience with your present law enforcement agency, what type(s) of training have you attended or been offered to assist officers with stress, depression, or thoughts of suicide?

17. How do administrators address the topic of law enforcement suicide within your department?

18.   How can administrators assist in reducing the high number of law

enforcement suicides?

Interview questions were used to elicit officer perceptions of care by peers and

administration and about the influence of training on difficult law enforcement situations.

Perception influences belief systems, which in turn influence individual reality.

Perceptions are individually unique, and "every perception counts; very perception adds

something important to the experience" (Moustakas, 1994, p. 53). Perception was

relevant to memory and knowledge, as individual perceptions are stored in the memory,

and the individual attaches meaning to the incident. As additional information and

knowledge are stored, knowledge is modified about individual perception and must be re-

perceived. The process brings about new perspectives on past knowledge, and is a

culmination of old, the new, and the unknown information causing individuals to re-

perceive.

Data Collection

Data are collected using audio-recorded interviews. Before the interviews were

conducted, participants were required to read and return a signed informed consent form

(see Appendix B). Interviews began by asking demographic questions to help build a

rapport with participants.

Interviews were conducted until the point of data saturation. According to Boyd

(2001), data saturation occurred between 2 to 10 participants. Saturation is not a function

of the number of participants, rather a function to the emergence of common themes from

data (Boyd, 2001). By interviewing at least 20 law enforcement officers about

perceptions of care and training, the possibility exists of reaching saturation of common themes. Interviews lasted between 30 and 60 minutes each, with the exception of the first interview lasting 1 hour and 40 minutes. The time allotted for each interview allowed enough time for participants to answer questions fully and for themes to emerge from the data collected. Each interview was audio recorded with permission of each participant.

The phenomenological interview was a formal process of open-ended questions and comments, which invoke the lived experience of the study participant (Moustakas, 1994). Open-ended questions were asked, because open-ended questions invoke deeper questions, comments, and concerns relevant to the study and the researcher (Moustakas, 1994). The use of qualitative research may enhance the views of participants through general and broad questioning, in spite of being subjective and biased (Moustakas, 1994; Neuman, 2005). Limited amounts of literature exist about the phenomenon of law enforcement suicide. The trends associated with officer suicide do not appear to have specific variables, favoring the use of a quantitative type of research method.

Data were collected in the form of audio recordings, transcripts, and field notes. Data were analyzed using the NVivo® software. Themes were identified and recorded by the number of times each theme presents itself during the interview process.

Ngwenyama (2001) explained reduction of clustered groups and emerging themes into the simplest form was accomplished by asking two questions. First, does each statement contain something sufficient to constitute an understanding for it? (Ngwenyama, 2001). If yes, is it possible to reduce further the statement without violating the meaning of the statement presented by the participant? (Ngwenyama, 2001). The overall goal of data collection is to develop a deeper understanding of the lived experience of police officers about training's impact on difficult issues in law enforcement, more importantly, officer suicide.

Validity and Reliability

Validity and reliability are used to obtain objectivity and credibility (Kirk & Miller, 1986; Silverman, 2001). Neuman (2005) explained validity as an association of the phenomenon studied with what was actually written and recorded. If inadvertently the research includes or excludes more than the claimed phenomenon, overall validity weakens (Kirk & Miller, 1986; Neuman, 2005). A suggestion of truth exists between the identified constructs and the measurement of validity. The accretion of validity measures provides a foundation of evidence, which over time will provide substantial support (Neuman, 2005). The mere suggestion of truthfulness by way of the perfect instrument is suspect, due to limited accuracy (Kirk & Miller, 1986). Audio-recordings minimize error during interviews. Reliability and validity are each equally useful but each is proportioned differently. Triangulation is used to develop a deeper, more meaningful understanding of the collected evidence. Triangulation occurred using the interview, audio recordings, and field notes, all of which provided a diverse collection of information. Triangulation was used in order to form different viewpoints about emerging concepts, themes, and phenomenon. Emphasis is place on reliability because perfect validity is not theoretical obtainable (Kirk & Miller, 1986).

Internal validity.

Validity includes internal and external validity (Neuman, 2005). The overall credibility of a study determines validity (Neuman, 2005). High internal validity indicates few, if any, errors; low internal validity indicates a greater likelihood that errors will present themselves (Neuman, 2005). One way to establish internal validity of qualitative research is by triangulation. Triangulation involves the different viewpoints about concepts, themes, and phenomenon (Neuman, 2005).

According to Neuman (2005), four types of triangulation existed. The first type of triangulation involves numerous measurements of the phenomenon being researched (Neuman, 2005). The second type involves multiple research observers contributing to additional perspectives of the phenomenon (Neuman, 2005). The third type includes the implementation of theory in the beginning processes of the research (Neuman, 2005). The fourth type includes the utilization of both qualitative and quantitative research and data (Neuman, 2005).

The theory of triangulation occurs with the implementation of numerous perspectives of theory in the beginning of planning research (Neuman, 2005). Addressed in the study were officers' perceptions about mental health training on the incidence of officers' suicide and officers' perceptions of care by administration and peers during difficult personal situations. Because validity was not theoretically obtainable, personal interviews, audio recordings, and field notes were used to help identify themes regarding the studied phenomenon. The triangulation of the three means of collection contributed to numerous perspectives of the information collected. Audio recordings minimize errors in transcription or understanding (Moustakas, 1994).

External validity.

External validity allows the researcher to generalize research findings in any size group or setting (Neuman, 2005). The three types of agencies included in the study ranged in size from large (federal), to medium (county) to small (municipal) agencies.

Police culture is a concept, which is similar to many law enforcement agencies and officers. The ability to generalize the findings of the study may provide administration, instructors, and officers with important information, which may assist officers in dealing with stress, ultimately reducing the number of law enforcement suicides.

Police culture is a common practice within law enforcement communities worldwide, and a practice of a majority of police officers (Crank, 2004; Quinn, 2005). External validity is the ability to apply the workings of law enforcement culture from one specific department to a more encompassing number of police departments. External validity is primarily applied to experimental types of research and includes the ability to generalize the data collected (Neuman, 2005). If high external validity exists, the concept remains generalized to a larger group and context. Generalizability is low because of the small segment of the population or group being studied (Neuman, 2005).

Reliability.

Validity and reliability are important in all types of measurement, particularly given the ambiguous nature of social theory constructs (Neuman, 2005). A qualitative research study is reliable if the behaviors and actions can be replicated under similar conditions (Silverman, 2001). The focus of qualitative research is on observations of the presence or absence of phenomenon. The focus of quantitative research is on the number of times something occurs or does not occur (Kirk & Miller, 1986). No degree of symmetry exists between reliability and validity (Kirk & Miller, 1986). Reliability refers to the extent to which results are "independent of accidental circumstances of the research" (Kirk & Miller, 1986, p. 20). The use of audio recorded interviews and field notes increase the reliability of the data collection process and the research results.

Pilot Study

A pilot study was conducted to validate the research questions, which are included in the study. The pilot study involved the participation of 2 law enforcement officers from the population of law enforcement officers within Saint Louis County, Missouri. The pilot study respondents are not included in the final study and had no involvement or contact with any study participants. According to Creswell (2005), a pilot study is conducted by a small number of participants and requires participants to evaluate the validity of the instrument. Participant suggestions are evaluated and if appropriate, the changes are implemented into the final research instrument.

Data Analysis

The phenomenological analysis process involved organizing and analyzing the collected data. The process involved horizontalization of data such that each statement revealed through the interview process will have "equal value" (Moustakas, 1994, p. 118). Interviews were audio recorded and transcribed verbatim. Transcribed data was analyzed using the NVivo® software. NVivo® software assisted in the identification of common emerging themes from the audio recordings and field notes. The software minimized many of the labor-intensive tasks associated with data collection and analysis. The software extracted statements from the audio recordings and field notes. Data were extracted using general statements of participants and all information is useful. Extracted information was placed into clusters or groups, displaying repetition of common emerging themes.

Data analysis occurred through the use of NVivo ® software and the modified van Kaam method developed by Moustakas (1994). Data analysis assisted in better understanding the lived experience of law enforcement officers about perceptions of the impact of training on the incidence of police suicide. The first step in data analysis is the *epoche* process (Moustakas, 1994). Epoche is a Greek term meaning to abstain from opinion or personal judgment (Moustakas, 1994). The use of the epoche process allows for clarity and purpose.

The second step is transcendental phenomenological reduction. Reduction involves organizing data to transcend the perception of everyday experiences by identifying things that appear to be witnessed for the very first time. Transcendental phenomenology helps explain simple phenomenon (Moustakas, 1994). Interview questions elicited answers and explanations to the questions asked; the collected words form common themes. The process of reduction helped reduce the phenomenon to the simplest form (Moustakas, 1994). The phenomenon of law enforcement suicide was a collection of officer perceptions about mental health training on the incidence of officer suicide and perceptions of care by peers and administration. Themes were part of the whole phenomenon of law enforcement suicide. Grouping themes helped identify common perceptions about the incidence of officer suicide.

Coding procedures combine manifest and latent content coding techniques. Manifest content refers to the capture of data from interactions that appear to have a deeper more meaningful intent (Maxfield & Babbie, 2005). Latent coding involves capture of conversational responses, which were not merely yes and no questions, rather questions requiring participants to divulge more information or to attach meaning to answers.

The focus of the data collected was on the phenomenon of law enforcement suicide, and perceptions of law enforcement officers about training's impact of officer suicide. The research question was *What are the lived experiences and perceptions of law enforcement officers concerning perceptions of care and the effect of training on difficult law enforcement issues and the incidence of suicide among law enforcement officers?* The purpose of the study was to explore the perceptions of the lived experiences of law enforcement officers about perceptions of care by administrators and peers and about the influence of mental health training on the incidence of officer suicide. Observation and communications by study participants allows for structural analysis of the information and insight gained. Seidel (1998) explained coding involved noticing, collecting, and thinking. Noticing is discovering things in the data, which appear important and coding that data, such as the use of field notes and audio recordings (Seidel, 1998). Collecting involves the act of physically collecting the data, and thinking involves thinking about the things, which were noticed and collected.

During coding, audio records were transcribed in order to notice terms and themes, which emerge and may be redundant. Themes possess values using alphabetical or numerical categories. Collecting was the process of extracting the data from field notes, audio recordings, and transcriptions. Thinking entails making sense of the data and information being collected, establishing emerging patterns or associations with each theme and across themes. Thinking entails making general observations about the themes in comparison to the phenomenon being researched (Seidel, 1998).

According to QSR International (2008), themes emerge in the nodes, which emerge through the materials (i.e. interviews and audio recordings). Interviews of individual officers allowed individual perceptions to contribute to emerging themes.

Classification of themes that emerge will be tree or free nodes. Tree nodes are "nodes

that are catalogued in a hierarchical structure, moving from a general category at the top

(the parent node) to more specific categories (child nodes)" (QSR International, 2008, p.

11). Free nodes are nodes that are separate from tree nodes, in the sense that these nodes

"have no clear logical connection with other nodes—they do not easily fit into a

hierarchical structure" (QSR International, 2008, p. 11). The emergence of themes

allows the data collection process to be minimally invasive.

To minimize researcher bias of common themes and observations, the researcher

exhibits impartiality regarding bias of common themes and prejudices (Miyazaki &

Taylor, 2008). Inaccurate recording can lead to biases being developed and can influence

the researcher or the individual's external environment in some way (Miyazaki & Taylor,

2008). Phenomenological research emphasizes the experience of the individual, not what

the researcher perceives. The borrowing of reflections and experiences supports a

meaning of deeper understanding with minimal bias (van Manen, 1990).

Summary

The data collected for the phenomenological qualitative research study provided

insight into the complex phenomenon of law enforcement suicide. Data consisted of the

perceptions of 20 White, male officers from municipal, county, and federal law

enforcement agencies within Madison and Saint Clair Counties in Illinois, and Saint

Louis County, Missouri, about perceptions of care and the impact training had on

difficult personal issues (i.e., depression, mental illness, or law enforcement officer

suicide) are uncovered in the data. Data were audio-recorded during the interview process and field notes, and transcribed with the use of the NVivo® software. Vital information and knowledge for future studies about the importance of life and the ability to save lives through training is addressed in the qualitative phenomenological study.

More law enforcement officers take their own lives than are killed in the line-of-duty (Violanti, 2007; Violanti & Samuels, 2007). Since officers committed suicide more frequently than were killed in the line of duty (Hackett & Violanti, 2003); the population was interviewed to gain a better understanding of perceptions and beliefs about why officers are taking their own lives. Law enforcement culture binds officers together. Law enforcement officers share a unique relationship in which one may risk their life for another without hesitation or question. Law enforcement personnel understand the struggles and intimate details of the lives of their peers, but often do not discuss such knowledge out of respect to fellow officers and the Code of Silence. The Code of Silence allows officers to remain apprised of happenings to peers, administrators, and departmental changes (Crank, 2004). The ability to interview the selected population may provide insight about the law enforcement community about the possible impact of training on the incidence of officer suicide. Officers' perceptions of mental health issues may provide insight into whether training increases skills necessary to deal with difficult personal situations.

Chapter 3 contained a discussion of the methodology for a phenomenological research method. Phenomenology is the study of the lived experience (van Manen, 1990). The appropriateness for the study was described in the relationship to the research problem, purpose, and theoretical framework. The lived experiences of law enforcement officers about the incidence of officer suicide may provide insight into reasons why officers commit suicide. Reliability and the validity of the research instrument, including an in-depth analysis of the instrument were discussed in chapter 3.

Chapter 4 includes descriptive statistics of the population sample. Chapter 4 includes an in-depth exploration of officer perceptions about training's impact on the incidence of law enforcement suicide. With the assistance of NVivo® software, themes are extracted from interview responses in an attempt to saturate the population with common themes. Common themes, which may provide insight into reasons why law enforcement officers are taking their lives faster than they are being killed in the line-of-duty. Chapter 4 concludes with a report of the data collected from each research question.

Chapter 4: Results

The purpose of the study was to explore the lived experiences of law enforcement officers concerning perceptions of care by administrators and peers and the influence of mental health training on the incidence of officer suicide. Provided in chapter 4 is a documentation of data analysis and collection procedures using the Modified van Kaam method introduced by Moustakas (1994). Also provided in chapter 4 is an in-depth explanation of participant demographics, research processes, and a detailed response by individual participants about the research questions presented. The research question addressed was *What are the lived experiences and perceptions of law enforcement officers concerning the effects of Police Suicide Awareness (PSA) training on the incidence of suicide among law enforcement officers?* Interviews were conducted with 20 White, male law enforcement officers to explore common themes about personal experiences of these officers about factors, which may contribute to law enforcement suicide.

Data collection involved a Modified van Kaam method of semi-structured in-depth interviews consisting of open-ended questions. Participant interviews were digitally recorded and transcribed to maintain internal validity. Audio recordings and transcripts were read several times each to develop an in-depth understanding of the lived experience of interview participants.

Data were grouped into clusters and further separated by meaning. The emerging clusters were analyzed through textural and structural descriptions as suggested by Moustakas (1994). Textural descriptions "Include verbatim examples from the transcribed interviews" (Moustakas, 1994, p. 121). Structural descriptions include the textural description and "the meanings and essences of the experiences, incorporating the invariant constituents and themes" (Moustakas, 1994, p. 121). Emerging themes were identified using the modified van Kaam (Moustakas, 1994) method and the NVivo 8® software (QSR International, 2009).

Data were grouped into categories based on major and minor themes and by identifiable patterns. Data collection continued until information saturation or information redundancy was reached. The entire interview process lasted approximately 5 weeks due to participant hesitancy of the topic; police suicide. Participant interviews were gauged at 30-45 minutes. All interviews met the qualifications, except the first interview, which lasted 100 minutes.

Chapter 4 includes a detailed analysis of 20 in-depth interviews of law enforcement officers from Madison and Saint Clair Counties in Illinois and Saint Louis County, Missouri. A pilot study consisting of 2 law enforcement officers was conducted. The officers involved with the pilot study did not have any contact with the study participants and were not included in the final study. Pilot study participants were used to test the validity of the research questions and to address content issues with research questions. The selected pilot study participants were chosen based on the same criteria of actual study participants.

Chapter 4 contains a description of the research findings from an analysis of the collected data. The qualitative phenomenological study consisted of 7 demographic questions and 18 interview questions regarding law enforcement officer perceptions of preventative suicide training programs and perceptions of care by peers and administrators. Chapter 4 includes a comprehensive description of the data collection results and an analysis of the collected data.

Assumptions

Five assumptions exist regarding law enforcement suicide. First, an assumption exists that rigorous background checks involved in the law enforcement hiring process will reduce or eliminate individuals who may be more susceptible to depression, stress, posttraumatic stress disorder (PTSD), and individuals who may be at an increased risk for suicide or suicidal behaviors (Hackett & Violanti, 2003; Violanti, 2007). The second assumption relays the message that law enforcement personnel are secretive about the topic of law enforcement suicide (Hackett & Violanti, 2003). The third assumption is that the secretive nature of law enforcement personnel regarding law enforcement suicides causes many law enforcement suicides to be classified as accidental, or misclassified for purposes of shame and survivor insurance benefits (Violanti, 1995). The fourth assumption is that there was a lack of discussion on the topic of law enforcement suicide (i.e., training and open communication) thus the message law enforcement personnel receive is that law enforcement suicide does not exist, and there is no problem (Violanti, 2007). The fifth assumption is that officers who commit suicide should not have been in law enforcement or that these officers were not mentally stable (Hackett & Violanti, 2003).

Pilot Study

The pilot group commented on the content of the interview questions, the wording of the interview questions, and any misunderstandings associated with any of the interview questions. Participant responses were used to evaluate instrument validity in terms of lucidity and significance. The pilot study consisted of 2 White, male law enforcement officers from departments within Saint Louis County, Missouri. The officers involved in the pilot study matched the inclusion criteria for the research study. The two officers in the pilot group are not included in the actual study and had no contact with any of the officers involved in the study. The police officers involved in the pilot meet study participant requirements. Pilot study participants averaged 38 years of age and were sworn full-time law enforcement officers with an average of 7 years of law enforcement experience. For the purpose of the narrative, references to the officers involved in the pilot study are Officer A and Officer B.

The significance of the pilot study led to demographic question number 7 being reworded. Demographic question number 7 stated, "How many years have you been a sworn full-time law enforcement officer." Officer B explained the question should have included the word "commissioned," because some law enforcement positions are not sworn, but rather commissioned positions. Demographic question number 7 was reworded to state: "How many years have you been a sworn or commissioned law enforcement officer?"

Study question number 4 stated, "Based on your experience with your present law enforcement agency, in what ways do you feel cared for by your peers?" Both pilot study participants could not provide an answer for this question. Officer A stated the question was too "touchy feely," and would be better stated with the word well-being. Study question number 4 was reworded as: "Based on your experience with your present law enforcement agency, in what ways do your peers show concern about your overall well-being?"

The change to interview question number 4 precipitated the change to interview questions 5 and 6. Interview question 5 stated, "Based on you experience with your present law enforcement agency, how does the care provided by administrators differ from the care by peers?" Interview question 5 was reworded to state: "Based on your experience with your present law enforcement agency, in what ways do you feel cared for by the law enforcement administration?"

Interview question 6 stated, "Based on your experience with your present law enforcement agency, how does the care provided by administrators differ from the care provided by peers?" Both officers explained the word care should be changed to concern. Interview question 6 was reworded to state: "Based on your experience with your present law enforcement agency, how does the concern provided by administrators differ from the concern provided by peers?"

Officer A explained that the term care was not the way he communicated with peers or with leadership. Further explaining men are seen as strong and the idea of showing feeling is like sharing a personal weakness. Officer A explained the tough exterior was further emphasized throughout the career of all law enforcement officers. Officer A went on to explain he was not concerned with whether officers cared about him. Officer A said, "At the end of the day there is really only a small group of people who really care about you, and that you care about." Officer A could not name one way in which he believed his peers showed that they cared about him or his well-being, but proceeded to share intimate details about the suicide of a fellow officer.

Officer A explained the background of the officer who committed suicide and he showed a real sense of hurt about the thought of a fellow worker even seeing suicide as an option. Officer A explained that numerous precipitating events led to the suicide, including relationship issues, alcohol, and bad judgment. Officer A explained that the way leadership handled the situation set the precedence for how officers were expected to act. Officer A explained fellow officers were not allowed to wear mourning bands over their badges and they were not allowed to utilize a department vehicle to escort the hearse to the cemetery. Officer A stated that, "Even before the body was cold, the dead officer's [work] locker was cleaned out." Officer A said administrators displayed a lack of empathy for the deceased officer, the officer's family, and the officer's peers.

Demographics

The selected study population was chosen because of the high incidence of suicide within the law enforcement population. Approximately 81% of all law enforcement positions are filled by Whites (Aamodt & Stalnaker, 2001); and approximately 89% of all law enforcement positions are filled by males (Aamodt & Stalnaker, 2001). According to the CDC (2005), White males between 35 and 54 years of age account for the second highest number of suicides in the United States, second only to elderly White males. The selected study participant population was chosen randomly from participating law enforcement agencies within Madison and Saint Clair Counties in Illinois, and Saint Louis County, Missouri. Ten study participants were from Madison County, Illinois; 9 of the study participants were from Saint Louis County, Missouri, and 1 study participant was from Saint Clair County, Illinois. All study participants were White male and all 20 participants held the title of police officer. According to the CDC (2005) description, the study population matches the segment of the population deemed high-risk for suicide. The average age of all study participants is

43 years of age, with the average number of years in law enforcement as a sworn or commissioned officer totaling 18 years.

Findings

Suicide is an epidemic that claims approximately 30,000 lives each year in the United States (CDC, 2005; Satcher, 1999). Suicide is more prevalent within intricate subcultures, such as law enforcement (Kelly & Martin, 2006; Violanti et al., 2007). Approximately 300-500 police officers commit suicide each year (Kelly & Martin, 2006; Violanti et al., 2007). More officers are killed by their own hand then are killed at the hands of others, making suicide the leading cause of death for police officers nationwide (Violanti et al., 2007). "Death by one's own hand is far too much a final gathering of unknown motives, complex psychologies, and uncertain circumstances— and it insinuates itself far too corrosively into the rights and fears and despairs of the living" (Jamison, 1999, p. 26).

The purpose of the qualitative phenomenological study was to explore the perceptions of the lived experiences of law enforcement officers about perceptions of care by administrators and peers about the influence of mental health training on the incidence of officer suicide. According to Jamison (1999):

Suicide is not an entirely private act, however; nor is it completely idiosyncratic or unpredictable. We have ways of understanding the psychological underpinnings of suicide, and while they may not provide the final clarity we would like, they give us grounds for a beginning. (p. 74)

Data were gathered and analyzed, producing the following major themes: *stress, humor, trust, training,* and *change.* The following minor themes emerged *generational issues* and *organizational administration.*

Interview question 1.

What are some of the most difficult situations you've encountered in your law enforcement career? Officers involved in the study listed more than one difficult situation in their careers but the following percentages show which item the officer perceived as being the most difficult situation to them personally. Ten of the 20 officers explained that the most difficult situations they faced in their law enforcement career were calls involving children (i.e., accidents, abuse, and death of children). Six of the officers mentioned the second most difficult situations participants encountered included being shot at, being involved in a shooting situation, and having to kill someone in the line-of-duty. One officer emphasized the most difficult situations encountered included mobile pursuits, foot pursuits and active fighting situations. Three of the 20 officers explained the most difficult situations encountered included traffic accidents, suicides, rapes, homicides, and any other type of disturbance.

Interview question 2.

Based on your experience with your present law enforcement agency, what types of training have you received regarding difficult law enforcement issues? Seven of the 20 officers stated they received minimal types of training. The 7 officers explained that the academy was foundational for their careers but there has been no more initiative by themselves or their departments to continue training on issues affecting law enforcement. Officer 7 explained "we get a lot of training on the victims and how to talk to the victims, other than that there is no training." Officer 17 mentioned he had only received minimal training from his current department, explaining that most of his training was received while in the military.

Six of the 20 officers added they received adequate training in the following areas: basic investigations, breathing techniques, child pornography, child sexual abuse, domestic abuse, firearms, ground fighting, homicide investigation, interviewing techniques, law and procedure pursuit training, scenario-based training, sexual abuse cases, shooting drills, substance abuse. Officer 3 stated:

> As far as dealing with the way these issues make you feel when you go home, I have never received anything for this. You definitely look at your kids different when you go to a traffic crash or a scene where there are pictures and stuff of the little guys your kids' age. It takes you a little while to get back to being a dad.

Four of the 20 officers explained they receive some type of monthly training either in-service or on CD-ROM, in regards to dealing with issues they face specifically within their departments. Officer 5 explained, "You cannot try to train someone to drive 70 mph in traffic, chasing a bad person who just shot someone, you cannot recreate that." Officer 2 stated:

> We are always geared about helping everyone else, but very rarely do we worry about taking care of ourselves. We are in law enforcement to help everybody else but we need to help ourselves out. Studies show fire, cops, and EMS, after about 3-4 years they say they don't want to do this anymore.

Three of the 20 officers stated they received adequate training, but further stated that the only foundational training they had received was in the police academy. Officers

1, 10, and 11 stated they were able to recall things they had been told in the academy that they believed to be important to them personally or professionally. Officer 10 explained, "I remember my instructors alluding to the fact that police work is difficult for the family, but never remember them saying this is how to get through it." Officer 1 acknowledged everything is a regurgitation of the academy, "there's really nothing new, it's just giving it to you again and it's coming from your own experience." Officer 1 noted a conversation he had with a rookie officer about being in a true knock down drag out fight. Officer 1 stressed that many of the officers joining the force today have never been in a real fight, stating:

> Have you been sprawled out on the front of your cat fighting with a guy, getting ready to run out of energy, and praying that here comes the second officer? You're not gonna [sic] teach me how to fight with somebody; I've been there, I've been in that fierce situation and you haven't, but their position is that now they are subject-matter experts that are trying to teach me.

Interview question 3.

Based on your experience with your present law enforcement agency, how do you believe the provided training was useful? Ten of the 20 officers felt the training received was useful. Officers believed training helped to alleviate their fears, to calm them down, raised awareness, and to provide insight into the issues they were being trained on but the training provided to law enforcement has never been specifically tailored to law enforcement. Officer 10 emphasized training is a premium within his department but explained training is looked at favorably and is highly encouraged by all officers within the department. Officer 10 also added that "officers are encouraged to get specialized training, but training regarding mental health and stress are overlooked, not just within his department but in all departments." Officer 10 attributed the issues cops face to issues of life expectancy after a career in law enforcement. As a law enforcement instructor, Officer 10 likes to bring the reality home to new recruits, by stating:

You retire at 50 and you're dead by 59 and that's not good. I think this has to do with officers burying their problems in alcohol and a bucket of chicken wings, rather than talking things out with anybody. I think officers are better at this now but I don't think we are anywhere where we need to be. We need people from within the field to help; it is frowned upon and not given priority.

Officer 6 indicated in the following excerpt that he felt the training he received prepared him to be a better counselor than a cop. Officer 6 stated:

As a cop you don't have three hours to talk somebody down, and as much as I hate to admit it; this training was good on working with people with mental health issues. Over time I have a whole bag of dirty tricks.

Officer 11 explained that, "training can help prepare the framework but that training doesn't even touch the surface, because nothing can compare to actually doing it."

Ten of the 20 officers believed that the training they received regarding difficult law enforcement issues was not adequate. Officer 14 concluded that the training provided looks good on paper, but in reality, the training is not functional. Interview question 4 was developed to address training issues at the officer's current department. All of the participating officers received academy training and additional specialized training but the responses are based on their currently employing agency.

Interview question 4.

Thinking back on the training you received, what could have been improved to increase the effectiveness of the training? Thirteen of the 20 officers mentioned there was nothing in their opinions that could have been improved to increase the effectiveness of the training. Seven of the 20 officers added that the following things could be used to improve the overall effectiveness of the training they have received: more verbal judo, new instructors, new tactics and procedures, more role-playing, have a better foundational understanding of mental health issues, having pro cop instructors, and ways to deescalate stressful situations. Officer 6 best summarized the experiences of the officers by stating that the generational differences can be seen in the older officers, when compared to the new officers joining the force. Officer 6 explained "I handle things differently from these guys, and part of it is the culture. It is okay for guys to cry and wear pink, give me a break. I am still of the opinion that men should be men." Officer 6 further explained that even though he is much older than many of the officers in the department, he has the real life experience which is what he says keeps officers alive. Officer 6 noted:

> I am one of two guys in the department who are kind of considered dinosaurs. I have done a lot of things in my life, other than be a cop. I like helping people, but some of the things we get calls for are ridiculous. I see things differently than a lot of guys, because many of these guys come straight out of college. I have life experience. We are really glorified referees and we get paid well for the little work we do. In actuality, a 12-hour shift is 11 hours and 59 minutes of sheer

mind numbing boredom and one minute of abject sheer terror. And personally, that is what I live for, I am an adrenaline junkie.

Interview question 5.

Based on your experience with your present law enforcement agency, in what ways do your peers show concern for your overall well-being? All participating officers indicated that they felt peers showed concern for their overall well-being no matter how insignificant, in the following ways: showing a real sense of concern, asking if they need to talk, giving each other crap, joking around, humor, camaraderie, if something is out of character they will inquire, showing support for individual officers and their family, cursing, sharing stories, we go out for supper or drinks, and an overall show of teamwork. Officer 16 stated, "We do look out for each other. We may not always get along, but when it comes to the job we always back each other up completely and make sure that we all go home safely at the end of the day." Officer 4 emphasized "I have three rules, Rule 1: I go home at the end of every shift. Rule 2: My crew goes home at the end of every shift, and Rule 3: There's no changing Rule 1 or Rule 2."

Officer 3 emphasized that friendships are established over times with the guys from your crew and it is a special sort of bond, in which when you know you belong, everything is just right in the world. Officer 1 explained the idea of having a few very close friends in which he believed he could share anything with, personal or professional. Further stating that sometimes "you are just being buddies" (Officer 1) and you want to joke around and other times there are real serious issues in which you turn to your close-knit group of friends. Officer 1 stated there are the friends who you can cry in front of and spill your heart out to, and know that they will not share this with the rest of the group or use it to try to hurt you with your peers. Officer 3 mentioned that there is an issue if your peers stop joking with you or giving you crap. In the following excerpt, Officer 10 compared the police family to a dysfunctional family, in that the police family protects each member of the family but oftentimes, the family is the cause of many of the issues facing the individual:

> We are a family, a dysfunctional family, with the focus on dysfunction. The law enforcement family, like most families will come together around an officer who needs help, but as with our own families, if the officer doesn't come out and ask for help they don't get it. They say I guess he's okay and this causes isolation. He doesn't want to ask for help because he fears others will think he is weak, or will show weakness. This department and every other department functions like this.

Officer 10 explained that he had recently been promoted and was feeling a tremendous amount of personal and professional stress. Officer 10 stated that his promotion has placed him in an administrative role in which he feels extremely isolated from his peers. Officer 10 further added that he went to a gathering at a local bar for a peer and when he walked up to the table everyone stopped talking. Officer 10 relayed that his recent promotion placed him in the category of administration and this movement had taken away the past trust he built with peers. Officer 10 further explained "it was because he was in the "us" versus "them" game now. The "us" versus "them" is how line officers communicate issues among themselves and those individuals in administrative roles."

Interview question 6.

Based on your experience with your present law enforcement agency, in what ways does administration show concern about your overall well-being? Twelve of the 20 officers concluded that administrators showed minimal if any concern for their overall well-being. Eight of the officers believed their administrators showed some degree, no matter how minimal for their overall well-being. Officer 8 concluded that his administrators were there to take your gun away, stating that they take care of you through hospitalization and counselors. Officer 14 added that his administrators "do the bare minimum to keep the paperwork straight for yearly requirements, but other than that, they could care less as long as someone shows up to fill a slot." Officer 7 felt administrators were more concerned about their personal matters, to extend any kind of concern to the officers. Officer 1 elaborated on this concept, by stating he was told by his Chief upon hiring: community first, department second, and officer third. Officer 1 indicated that this really affected his perceptions of how administration viewed him as a person and how he felt that they lacked a true concern for his overall well-being. Officer 1 stated, "They say that they care as a general rule, but they are more worried about themselves and the department's appearance, and how you look, as part of the department than how you truly are."

Officers 16 and 20 mentioned that their administrators showed concern for the officers by implementing a wellness program, encouraging working out, losing weight, and balancing mental and physical well-being. Officer 18 noted that he felt administrators showed concern for him by asking about his family. Officer 4 explained he was involved in a shooting and he felt a true sense of concern by administration because they showed up on the scene and asked if he needed anything.

Interview question 7.

Based on your experience with your present law enforcement agency, how does the concern provided by administration differ from the concern provided by peers? Thirteen of the 20 officers discussed the concern provided by administrators was seen as a formal type of relationship which involved filling slots, doing paperwork, and limiting issues of liability, whereas their peers were authentically concerned about each other. Six of the 20 officers emphasized that although the concern by administrators was not at the level of their peers, they did not feel as though there really was a difference between the concern provided by administrators or peers. Officer 15 indicated that he had not been at his current agency long enough to see if there really was a difference between the concern exhibited by administrators and his peers.

Interview question 8.

Based on your experience with your present law enforcement agency, what have you learned through training concerning the signs and symptoms of stress and depression? Eleven of the 20 officers stated they have not received any type of training concerning the signs and symptoms of stress and depression. One department had an officer suicide and still no training was provided to educate the other officers on the signs and symptoms of stress and depression (Officer 13). Eleven of the 20 officers noted they had received some type of training, which covered the basics of stress and depression but no training was specifically tailored to the law enforcement community.

Four officers were part of the 40-hour state certification Critical Incident Team in which officers are trained to deal with people who are depressed, suicidal, and individuals suffering from numerous types of mental illness. Critical Incident Team training is aimed at recognizing the signs and symptoms before there is a fatality, and to use the resources available to assist individuals in seeking help through hospitalization or counseling. Officer 1 wished he would have had the CIT class when he first became a cop. Officer 5 mentioned that there was a small section in the training which discussed law enforcement suicide, but cops are good at hiding it, but it would be difficult, because "It is part of our makeup to look for things that are out of place." Five officers said they knew several of the signs of stress and depression, but were unable to articulate more than a personal knowledge of the signs and symptoms.

Interview question 9.

In your opinion or experience, what is the effect of training, if any, on stress and depression in officers? Twelve of the 20 officers emphasized that in their opinion or experience that training had little if any effect on stress and depression in officers. Eight officers stated that in their opinion or experience, training had some degree of effect of the levels of stress and depression witnessed in officers. The number one effect was the ability of officers to be more aware of their surroundings. Officer 10 added "The problem is that we are being trained on such a broad spectrum anymore that it seems that the spectrum is being stretched all the time." The issue also came up about competing training and the lack of emphasis on officer well-being. Officer 11 indicated that he struggled with putting things into perspective. Adding he was finally able to decipher what he could and could not control, and what he could control he did (Officer 11).

Officer 3 explained besides the training he has received, he has a very good support system, to include his immediate family, extended family, peers, and his church.

Interview question 10.

What attempts do you make to minimize stress and depression in yourself?
Eleven of the 20 officers confirmed they attempted to minimize stress and depression in themselves by spending time with family and friends and maintaining connections with the world outside law enforcement. The world outside law enforcement includes: hunting, fishing, shooting, working out, weight lifting, and spending time alone. Eight officers stated they use humor and joking as a way to minimize stress and depression personally and professionally. One officer concluded that he was not successful in his ability to minimize or even control his stress and depression. Officer 10 stated "I have a new job and a lot of things on my plate. I can barely keep up. I think there will be a time when this changes but for right now it is really difficult. I used to deal with it by working out and lifting." When asked if Officer 10 had anyone similar in rank to talk to, he stated he did not and elaborated to state:

> No, I'm kind of in Siberia right now, and I know that sounds like a crazy way to
> put it, but all my life I have been a patrol officer or a sergeant of patrol or a
> detective. All those things are focused on police work and now that I have been
> promoted, it is all about management and not police work.

Officer 10 went on to explain how isolated he felt from his former peers and how they would joke around asking him if he counted all his paperclips today. In response, Officer 10 noted:

This is well meaning, but I have to deal with the internal strife right now, and it is a headache and stressful right now. I see light at the end of the tunnel, it's eating at me, but it's a long tunnel. I realize I am in the position I am in because I need to be here. Either the position will change and will be more manageable for me, or the person who moves into this position will have the benefit of my pain. I don't think there is any maliciousness in this department, but what it comes down to is this department has changed so quickly and the mission so rapidly that we all have been thrown in the deep end of the pool. The stress level is really high and it is hard to deal with the stress. Wearing the hat I wear really has an isolating effect.

While talking with Officer 10, the sincerity in his words and the perceived strife from his new promotion appeared to outwardly affect his demeanor. The effects or perceived effects of the isolation Officer 10 discussed seemed to be taking a toll. After interviewing Officer 10, concerns were raised about perceptions of care and his personal ability to deal with what he referred to as "surmounting stress" in conjunction with his new promotion.

Interview question 11.

What attempts do your peers make to minimize stress and depression in fellow officers? Twelve of the 20 officers noted that humor, joking, and talking were used as ways to minimize stress and depression among themselves and their peers. Humor and joking, according to Officer 4 are essential to police work, but stated "Officers have a tendency to not want to talk, especially male officers. It is our testosterone and ego. Men can't seem to be sensitive because our peers will think you are less than manly." In an attempt to appear manly or at a minimum, to not be perceived as less than manly, officers develop numerous types of protective mechanisms. Officer 4 explained:

> We joke around and share stories, you have to do that. We have a sick sense of humor, police officers do. You will learn and find out, even at the scene where someone was killed, to release the pressure, to not think much about it, we will joke. We make sure there are no family members or anybody is in earshot but we make crude jokes just to reduce the tension. It's stressful to us when stuff like that happens.

Officer 1 indicated that humor and joking are used to help officers bond and to help make a serious situation not seem so serious. Officer 1 related a story to reveal how officers use humor and bonding to protect each other and to lighten the mood. Officer 1 stated:

> When a cop wrecks a car it usually ends up with him buying a day off (i.e., a day off without pay). The officer buying the day off is worried about the repercussions of his actions, so his peers will make contact with them in order to let them know this kind of thing happens to everyone and they will make a joke about it, in attempt to help reduce the officer's stress.

Officer 1 noted he learned to get over many things by using a statement from his own dad, which stated, "They can kill ya [sic], but they can't eat ya [sic]."

Five officers indicated that they did not do anything to try to reduce stress of fellow officers. Through interactions with the community and administration, police officers learn to protect themselves and peers from outsiders. The police officers have the responsibility of confronting the public, in order to enforce the law; in-turn, the police officers are being judged by those they are to protect and serve. Crank (2004) explained the "thin blue line ... evokes the symbolic moral guardianship of the police" (p. 347). Crank (2004) explained police culture was an onion with three distinct layers. The layers include the street environment, uncertainty, and solidarity (Crank, 2004). According to Crank, the street environment included individuals with whom officers contributed much time (i.e., criminals and suspects). The layer identified as uncertainty includes the uncertain nature of police work, the uncertainty of each call an officer responds to, and the mere unpredictability of the unknown (Crank, 2004). The final layer of solidarity involves the protective mechanism officers use to protect themselves from outsiders (Crank, 2004). "Recognizing that cultural identity is often forged in conflict with other groups, this layer of the onion is seen as a product of the way in which the police view other groups with resentment and hostility" (Crank, 2004, p. 61).

As seen in the following excerpt from Officer 16, police officers are expected by the public to be strong and confident. Peers expect officers to portray competency in their jobs, but also to have an outward appearance of strength and courage. Officers cannot openly display emotion; those who choose to do so are judged harshly by peers. Police culture often dictates officer behavior (Crank, 2004). In-turn, officers who participate in the workings of the culture perpetuates the Code of Silence. Police culture does not accept the open display of emotion by officers, as seen in the following excerpt by Officer 16:

> If we see someone who is having problems we address the person, but officers
> have the tendency to not want to talk, especially male officers. It is our
> testosterone and ego. Men can't seem to be sensitive because your peers will

think you are less than manly.

Five officers mentioned they did not do anything to minimize stress and depression in fellow officers. Officer 5 observed departmental morale decreasing due to downsizing, budget deficiencies, manpower issues and the transferring of officers to other departments. Officer 5 further stated, "The department is having trouble getting morale back up. Everyone is burned out and I don't see it getting any better." Three officers indicated they tend to spend time with members of their crew off-duty (i.e., talking, movies, eating out, and playing golf) as a way to increase and maintain morale.

Interview question 12.

Based on your experience with your present law enforcement agency, in what ways do administrators strive to minimize officer stress and depression? Twelve officers noted that administrators in their present law enforcement agency did nothing to minimize stress and depression in their officers. Eleven of the 12 officers felt as though administrators actually went out of their way to increase officer stress levels. Eight officers believed administrators tried to reduce officer stress, if even minimally, in the following ways: allowing officers time to work out on duty, providing assistance to officers who may be having personal problems, they encourage off-duty activities, rotating assignments, officers are not micro-managed, education is provided, and providing a staffed psychologist for officers to talk to.

Interview question 13.

How do you feel that law enforcement contributes to stress and depression in officers? Eighteen of the 20 officers attributed the nature of the job to the majority of stress and depression in police officers. Officer 5 explained police officers deal with the negatives of society. "You deal with 10% of the population 90% of the time. You pick up this negative mindset, where everyone is bad. You have trouble picking out the good and the bad, this is difficult" (Officer 5).

The nature of the job includes the high-risk calls, adrenaline dumps, going for long periods doing absolutely nothing, and feeling as though you are constantly being judged by outsiders (Officer 1). Police officers work with the dark side of society and at times have to walk on the dark side themselves (Officer 9). Officer 11 stated:

> The job will consume you. It has me. I often tell young officers that this job has been a passion of mine since the first day I rode in a police car. I said I could not imagine not being a policeman. I don't know what I would have done. My whole family is blue collar. I love the excitement, the knowledge. I mean I know everything that goes on. I really do get a charge from making things right. I have always rooted for the underdog. I do it on a bigger scale now. I protect people who can't protect themselves.

Officer 1 told a story about his partner and himself doing CPR for 10 minutes, saving a man who turned out to be a crack head. Officer 1 became upset when the next call he had was an elderly man, who nearly died after just being released from the hospital. The range of emotion is constant with little if any time in between calls to be able to put things back into perspective.

Officer 6 emphasized law enforcement is a stressful job and that you have to expect this when you choose it as a career. Officer 6 further explained that stress had to be managed on an individual basis, by not allowing yourself to be adversely affected by every call taken, "otherwise you would be a basket case in less than a month." Officer 6 explained:

> Everybody's gonna [sic] die of something; nobody has left here on their feet. If
> you go to a car wreck and you can't handle the dead people, you may want to
> consider selling insurance. There's nothing wrong with selling insurance, but
> you're probably not gonna [sic] see a lot of dead people. I was told once, life is
> cheap and fragile, there's no rhyme or reason for death, so either get used to it or
> get out.

Officer 10 explained that a lot of the stress experienced in law enforcement comes from people identifying themselves by their job. Officer 10 concluded, "Young officers have a tendency to fall in love with the job and the excitement." Officer 16 explained law enforcement "starts out in a sort of fantasy about wearing the gun and the badge, but the truth is cops witness the underbelly of society." Officer 16 explained:

> I guess the best way to put it is firemen go to a call with a kitty cat in a tree. They
> get the kitty down out of the tree and everyone's happy. The problem with cops
> is they get the call for the kitty cat, but the kitty is not stuck in a tree, someone has
> killed the kitty cat. Now you've got to go and investigate why the kitty cat was
> killed. You don't get the joy but rather the pain of notifying the owner about his
> dead cat.

Officer 16 elaborated on the fact that police officers were often required to deliver terrible news (i.e., accident and death notifications). Officers are called when assistance is needed and often the only contact between the police and the community is initiated out of negative incidents.

Two officers believed law enforcement stress was increased by negative opinions of the public and press and by personal issues brought to the job. Officer 13 stated that he did not believe law enforcement culture acknowledged officer stress, depression, or suicide. The lack of acknowledgement by law enforcement culture produces a disconnect between how society views police work and how difficult police work can be on the individual officer. The lack of understanding between law enforcement and the general public contributes to a lack of trust and understanding about what police work entails, causing officers to feel isolated from outsiders, while in-turn building stronger more cohesive bonds with fellow officers. Crank (2004) explained that officers are expected to work in a number of different working environments and through the environments patterns are developed and cultural norms and behaviors are formed. "It is in the context of these environments, and the particular patterns by which the culture is articulated with the environments" (Crank, 2004, p. 65).

The public does not have the opportunity to work daily with the police over extended periods of time, but rather, they develop beliefs about the police through personal contacts with the police and what they see in the media (Crank, 2004). The concealment and misclassification of law enforcement suicides is an issue not shared openly with the public or the media. As stated by Officer 6, if officers believe they cannot turn to their fellow officers or administrators for help, they begin to feel isolated further by the beliefs and perceptions held by the general public. Officer 6's exact words were:

I don't perceive myself as having a problem … and if I did, I would never go there. You would be stigmatized. This place is unique in that it is too small to be big and too big to be small. We are small enough to know everyone and everybody's business.

Interview question 14.

How do you see the culture hindering officers seeking assistance for stress and depression? Sixteen of the 20 officers mentioned that law enforcement culture was still alive and well, and that the culture significantly hindered officers wishing to seek assistance for stress and depression. Officers 6, 16, and 19 said they would feel stigmatized by peers if they came forward, so in-turn, they would feel obligated to seek assistance outside their law enforcement circles. Officer 10 indicated officers were supposed to be warriors, who displayed a warrior mindset in which they are able to handle anything. If they cannot handle something they are perceived as weak or less than masculine by their peers (Officer 10). Perceptions of one's masculinity are influenced by police culture. According to Crank (2004), masculinity in police work had four broad themes: "the avoidance of anything vaguely feminine, the attainment of success and social status, a manly air of toughness, confidence, and self-reliance" (p. 231).

Officer 20 explained that the brotherhood of the badge used to signify keeping problems hidden or only sharing them with a partner and trying to work them out. Officer 20 observed the brotherhood mindset and explained the brotherhood is going to the wayside because of the rise of mental health issues facing law enforcement officers. Officer 14 stated, "You can't just go tell your partner you're feeling bad, it just doesn't work like that. No matter what he's going to give you trouble about it." However, Officer 14 noted the culture is making it easier for officers to come forward and believed if a fellow officer approached him he would be able to recognize quickly if this officer was truly struggling. Police culture instills in the officer that fear is not an emotion that should be displayed openly. Officer 1 shared a story about the outer image perceived in police culture. Officer 1 believed there was a double standard when it came to how stressful situations were handled by males and females:

> You and I are both cops, we have both been through a stressful situation, inside I am going man, she is holding up to this without showing any emotion. Man, inside I am torn up. She's holding up, I have to be like her. Especially when there's a woman around and so now, I have the added turmoil of I want to spill my guts out and perhaps just you being a female officer, I want to reach out and just lay my head on your shoulder and ball. There's that motherly comfort, which sounds retarded, yet at the same time, internally you are going I am in a man's world or in a stereotypical man's world, I can't show my weakness. I want to sit here and cry, but look at him, he's sitting here laughing and cracking jokes. When in actuality we both want to just sit down and either yell or scream, ball like babies, or throw a temper tantrum, but neither one of us will break the ice.

Officer 3 explained if he did have a call where he believed he needed professional assistance he would seek it on his own. He stated that seeking outside assistance could be denial, but he was never approached by administration to see if he was okay, so he just assumed he should be okay (Officer 3). Officer 3 stated he did not fear losing his job by coming forward, but rather losing the respect, credibility, and standing with his peers and administrators. Officer 3 further defended the way he handled the culture, by confiding in two very close police friends who he feels he could reveal anything. Officer

3 goes fishing with these two very close police friends, they discuss the issue at hand and the issue is never spoke of again or shared with spouses.

Officer 16 considered coming forward for help as the "kiss of death"; when in actuality, there was just a need to talk and get something off his chest. Officer 16 explained that losing trust and faith with peers was a paramount disappointment to the job. Officers talk about loose cannons (Officer 16). Peers will begin to question whether the loose cannon can do their job, or whether they will cower or get someone else hurt (Officer 16). The idea of an officer coming forward for help can result in the loss of employment, gun, badge, and arrest authority (Officer 16).

Four officers believed the culture was changing for the better (Officers 2, 9, 11, 19). Officer 8 elaborated by explaining the culture is becoming more open and accepting because officers and administrators know suicide is a real problem facing law enforcement. "We know guys are gonna [sic] come forward for help and we don't make fun or anything, we are as supportive as needed" (Officer 8). The Employee Assistance Program [EAP] is a program readily available to officers in many departments and their families. Employee Assistance Programs are typically used in conjunction with basic health insurance to provide officers with additional outlets to address problems (i.e., substance abuse, anger, counseling, depression), which may influence the officer's personal lives, work performance, or the officer's overall health. Employee Assistance Programs allow officers to utilize outside agencies without fear of repercussions and without the fear of being labeled by fellow officers. Officer 5 explained that his department has policies in place per the union contract, which allowed for time off and confidentiality of such issues. Officer 2 added that things are changing for the better. He stated in the past, in order to get hired, you had to be "the meanest, biggest, strongest, 250 pounds and you weren't gonna [sic] be hired if you didn't fit this description, you had to be able to beat everybody up and go home" (Officer 2). Officer 2 continued by noting the culture was changing and that things were "becoming more touchy feely." Officer 2 did not explain whether he thought this was a positive or a negative, but he explained that the generational differences between officers provide change, whether good or bad. Officer 2 explained:

> The culture is changing and the newer officers are what I consider the *thumb nation*. They are focused on immediate gratification. They are desensitized to the fighting, but they are more focused on problem-solving. The social faux pas is no longer there in regards to being a police officer and letting emotions show. These young guys now are looking for solutions and they are questioning things. The Code can foster into it but in my mind I think the Code does not control officers as much as we may think.

Interview question 15.

How do you see the culture influencing the acknowledgement of officer stress and depression? Sixteen of the 20 officers explained police culture was making positive changes in regards to acknowledgment of stress and depression in officers. The changes reported focused more on allowing officers to feel comfortable showing emotions and in coming forward if they need assistance. Officer 1 indicated that asking for assistance for mental health issues would jeopardize an officer's career, because mental health issues carry a stigma, which seemed impossible to erase. Officer 1 stated:

I think we will all openly say I'm pissed, grumpy, I'm down in the dumps but nobody would use that word [depressed]. That word is evil and it has a label, nobody wants to be labeled. I can come in and say I'm mad at the family, I'm mad at work, I hate my job, I hate my family and that's all accepted and well and good. That's normal macho guy stuff, but for me to just walk around kicking rocks as I'm walking that's not acceptable and you don't want to break that, they want to view you as stable and trusted.

The idea is you want to have the trust of peers but if someone is unstable, the secrets entrusted to them are now in question.

Officer 6 emphasized, "You open your mouth here, you better be sure because you can't get that genie back in the bottle. You screw up here and everyone will know about it." "There's an old saying, three can keep a secret if two are dead" (Officer 6). There is hesitancy in coming forward because officers do not want to face labeling by peers and administrators but they want to get better. The bond between officers within the culture is extremely powerful. Even if successful treatment is sought, the stigma attached the individual officer cannot be erased (Officer 6). Officer 10 explained that no one would come forward in the first minute of a conversation about the problems they are facing, and unless they reach out or behaviors would indicate a problem, such problems may never be known (Officer 10). "Unless there is some real clue there, we tend to miss it" (Officer 10).

Four officers believed that the culture does not acknowledge stress and depression in officers. Officer 16 stated that not only does the culture deny the realities of stress and depression in officers; the culture suppresses the issue and expects the same from officers. Officer 17 believed the culture denied issues of stress and depression in officers and the proof remains how an officer suicide within his department was handled. Officer 13 mentioned that the culture does not notice or understand the issues facing officers and the additional impact of a lack of empathy by the public. "I don't think the general public knows how rough this job can really be" (Officer 13).

Interview question 16.

Based on your experience with your present law enforcement agency, what type(s) of training have you attended or been offered to assist officers with stress, depression, or thoughts of suicide? Fifteen of the 20 officers verified that they received no training to assist them in dealing with stress, depression, or thoughts of suicide. The remaining five officers explained they received Critical Incident Training, which briefly covered the topics of stress, depression, and suicide in officers. Critical Incident Training includes a focus on the general population who suffer from stress, depression, and thoughts of suicide. Officer 4 explained if he had received any additional training, it was not significant enough to remember. Officer 16 stated he was told by administrators if he needed assistance with stress, depression, or thoughts of suicide he should seek assistance outside the department.

Interview question 17.

How do administrators address the topic of law enforcement suicide within your department? Nineteen of the 20 officers noted that administrators within their current departments have not addressed the topic of law enforcement suicide. One department actually had an officer suicide and according to Officer 13, administrators within his department tried to conceal this fact at all costs. Officer 13 stated that the mere denial of the suicide caused a back lashing of emotion from the officers and the local community. Officer 13 stated that the entire department was upset with how everything was handled. Officer 13 emphasized that no emails were sent out about the incident, officers were not allowed to wear mourning bands in observance of the officer, and officers were not allowed to use a department vehicle to escort the funeral procession. The mere fact that no policy existed was one issue, but the actions of administrators seemed to place the entire department in jeopardy. The abuse and misuse of trust between administrators and officers is still a sore subject even today (Officer 13). Administration within this department caused officer morale to plunge to unheard of levels, which is still apparent almost four years after the suicide (Officer 13). Officer 13 concluded that the officer suicide was only addressed once and was never discussed again.

Interview question 18.

How can administrators assist in reducing the high number of law enforcement suicides? Seventeen of the 20 officers explained that administrators could assist in reducing the high number of law enforcement suicides by paying more attention to officers, having sit down conversations about officer well-being, showing a minimal degree of concern for officers, opening up two-way communication, recognizing the signs and symptoms of law enforcement suicide, reducing the stigma attached to mental health issues, and providing specific education and training on the topics. Three officers stated they did not believe there was anything administration could do, because they believed that unless the person came forward, being able to know something was wrong would be extremely difficult. Officer 9 attributed suicide as an aspect of the job. Officer

9 explained there was an expectation of danger within certain professions. One profession in which danger is apparent is law enforcement.

Officer 9 stated:

There are certain jobs like in combat, where you have to assume a certain amount of risk. I deal with victims of crime who are good people and then I deal with the people who victimize them and they are horrible people. I just don't think there is anything you can do to prevent it or lower it. If you do this job right, it's gonna [sic] affect your marriage, your relationship with your children, it leads to divorce.

Thematic Results

Analysis of the data from the study participants resulted in the discovery of five major themes and two minor themes identified by study participants. Major themes include stress, stress relief, trust/loyalty, training, and change. The two minor themes include generational issues and organizational administration. Discussion of the themes appears in chapter 5.

The thematic results indicate areas that appear to be of significant importance to the officers interviewed. Police culture encompasses all of the major and minor themes that were discovered. The importance of addressing police culture is to assist society as a whole to understand better the role of law enforcement, to evaluate the need for police in society, and for those individuals in law enforcement to better understand how the culture helps and hinders their personal and professional development. Police culture is at the core of all thematic results and plays a significant role in the lives of law enforcement. In order to comprehend the daily struggles faced by law enforcement (i.e., stress, stress relief, trust/loyalty, training, change, generational issues, and organizational administration), it remains imperative to address the culture.

Summary

Provided in chapter 4 were insights about the perceptions of care by administrators and peers about issues affecting mental health training and officer suicide. The research included semi-structured interviews with 7 demographic and 18 research questions, which utilize the Modified van Kaam method introduced by Moustakas (1994). The Modified van Kaam method implored included a semi-structured interview of participants, which were digitally recorded, and ultimately transcribed.

Chapter 4 includes an in-depth explanation of participant demographics, research processes, and a detailed response by individual participants about the research questions presented. Emerging themes were identified based on officer perceptions. Based on the perceptions and explanations provided by officers numerous responses were provided as an explanation of the officer's interpretation of the research questions being presented.

Chapter 5 includes a summary of the study results captured through face-to-face interviews of 20 White, male police officers. Study results include the life experiences of law enforcement officers about perceptions of care by administrators and peers and about the influence of mental health training on the incidence of officer suicide. The discussion in chapter 5 includes the major themes identified in chapter 4 of stress, humor, trust, training, and change and the minor themes of generational issues and organizational administration. Chapter 5 concludes with an overview of study limitations, an in-depth discussion of major and minor themes recommendations for the population, recommendations for law enforcement administrators, and recommendations for future research.

Chapter 5: Conclusion and Recommendations

The purpose of the study was to explore the lived experiences of law enforcement officers concerning perceptions of care by administrators and peers and the influence of mental health training on the incidence of officer suicide. Participant interviews were conducted using the Modified van Kaam method introduced by Moustakas (1994). All face-to-face interviews were digitally recorded and transcribed for clarity and accuracy. Chapter 5 includes an overview of study limitations, an explanation of emerging themes, recommendations for the population, recommendations for law enforcement administrators, and recommendations for future research.

Limitations of the Study

Due to the sensitive nature of the research topic, participant willingness was nearly non-existent in Saint Clair County, Illinois. Letters of Inclusion (see Appendix C) were sent to 22 municipal agencies and 1 county agency. Of the 23 departments receiving letters of inclusion in Saint Clair County, no department heads agreed to participate and only 1 officer from an unnamed department chose to participate on an individual basis.

In Madison County, Letters of Inclusion were sent administrators of 21 municipal agencies, 1 county agency, and 1 state agency. Of the 21 agency administrators contacted in Madison County, only 3 agreed to participate. Several administrators and officers expressed concern over the topic of police suicide, the willingness to gain participation, and the overall honesty of officers agreeing to participate. Similar calls were received from individuals within Madison County, Illinois, which resulted in expanding the geographical location of the study into Saint Louis County, Missouri.

Due to a limitation in the willingness to participate, the geographical location of the study was extended into Saint Louis County, Missouri. Officers selected from agencies within Saint Louis County were selected using snowballing. Several officers located within agencies in Saint Louis County asked that they not be identified by department for fear of retaliation by administrators.

The following include the five major themes and two minor themes identified by study participants. Major themes include stress, stress relief, trust/loyalty, training, and change. The two minor themes include generational issues and organizational administration.

Major theme 1 stress.

Police work is a dangerous and stressful profession (Clark & Haley, 2007; Liberman et. al., 2002). Reuss-Ianni (1999) noted:

> One of the major results of the loss of a unifying culture in the department is the increasing evidence of organizational stress which affects police behavior. Police work has always been considered a high stress occupation with factors such as danger, violence, and erratic working hours causing serious problems for health and effectiveness. (p. 86)

A major source of stress for police officers occurs during times of trauma and prolonged exposure to daily calls, which never allows officer stress levels to decrease. Prolonged exposure to stressful types of incidents often results in what Clark and Haley (2007) referred to as a crisis:

> In a crisis, an individual's sense of psychological balance is disrupted by an adverse event or stressor. Most importantly, the individual's usual coping

mechanisms become temporarily ineffective. This leaves the individual potentially feeling overwhelmed, vulnerable, and/or agitated. In extreme circumstances, job performance and personal health may be impaired. (p. 1)

The number one major stressor for the police officers interviewed in the study included crimes involving children. Officer 3 explained that his stress increased with cases involving children, to include traffic accidents where children were hurt, domestic and substance abuse cases where children were not being taken care of and "sexual abuse cases are probably the most taxing things that a guy takes home with him at night." Officer 9 explained that he worked on a cyber crime task force and had to address copious cases of child pornography. Officer 9 stated that during his time on the task force, a major stressor included witnessing the death of an infant. Officer 10 stated the worst thing he had witnessed in his law enforcement career was viewing an autopsy of a 15-year-old boy. Crimes against children ranked as one of the most traumatic incidents witnessed by emergency personnel (Clark & Haley, 2007; Kirschman, 2007).

The second major stressor for the participants included officer-involved shootings. Officer-involved shootings include officers engaged in a gun battle between criminals, officer on officer shootings, and officer suicides (Crank, 2004). The members of the community expect officers to minimize crime and criminal activity, but officer on officer shootings are usually the result of mistaken identity. Officer suicide also involves the use of a gun, usually the officer's duty issued weapon, and the mere identification by fellow officers to the duty weapon seems to bring about additional stress. Officer 10 stated:

You are a cop 24 hours a day. Especially young officers, you fall in love with the job. There's a team atmosphere and it's exciting. After a while, the external stuff, like people from the outside butt heads, which is expected but the internal stuff is what causes stress. The internal stress is what wears people down.

Additional stressors included traffic accidents, vehicle and foot pursuits, divorce, conducting under-cover drug deals, testifying in court, homicide and suicide cases, being stabbed, hand-to-hand combat, rapes, and spousal abuse.

Waters and Ussery (2007) explained, "While not everyone in a hazardous profession exhibits discernible symptoms of stress immediately following a traumatic incident, in the long run, the cumulative impact of stress exacts its toll" (p. 172). Stressful life events are individualistic in nature, in which "some people are capable of ventilating their feelings and discharging their emotions, they don't suffer as much as others from stressful life events" (p. 172). Officers are not granted the privilege of the immediate release of emotion, placing them at greater risk for stress related disorders (Weisinger, 1985).

Officers are taught to control their emotions in order to remain in control of any situation. According to Blum (2000), the emotional scars left behind trauma often last long after the physical wounds have healed. Officers learn to conceal their emotions in an attempt to protect themselves from such stressful encounters (Blum, 2000). According to Karlsson and Christianson (2003), the mere socialization of officers to stressful events is seen in law enforcement culture as a rite of passage for young officers. Exposing officers to stressful events such as death "compels police officers to put a protective professional distance between themselves and certain aspects of their work, for instance their own fear of death" (Karlsson & Christianson, 2003, p. 420). When officers respond to the call of an abused child, they will often see the face of their own child, but the officer must remain composed and immune from reacting. Officers who fail to expose their weaknesses will often succumb to severe stress reactions, both at home and at work (Blum, 2000).

Major theme 2 stress relief.

Optimal mental health is a prerequisite to police work (Kelley, 2005). Compromised mental functioning can cause officers to "lose touch with the common sense and resilience they need to minimize stress, enjoy their work, and operate at peak performance" (Kelley, 2005, pp. 6-7). One way in which officers in the study relieve stress is through the sharing of stories and humor. Fifteen of the 20 officers emphasized humor was a major part of police culture and explained they used humor as a way to relieve stress and to bond with fellow officers. Additional stress relief tactics included weight lifting, meditation, watching movies, golfing, and eating breakfast together as a shift.

Cultures such as law enforcement, which exhibit hours of mind numbing boredom and moments in which officers face life and death situations, cause the collective to reinforce the values of the culture (Crank, 2004). Officers use humor in an attempt to manage the moments of boredom and terror (Crank, 2004). Police humor is often dark and often revolves around scenes involving death and human misery. Officers often gather to tell jokes and stories about a scene or an incident, as a way of dealing with the incident. Officer 4 noted that officers were human, but that the officers used coping mechanisms, which the culture deems appropriate:

We joke around and share stories. You have to do that. We have a sick sense of humor, police officers do. You will learn and find out, even on a scene where someone was killed, to release the pressure, to not think about it, we will joke. We make sure there are no family members or anybody in earshot, but we make crude jokes just to reduce the tension. It is stressful on us when stuff like that happens.

Officer 1 stated a common area of humor was an officer getting in trouble. Officer 1 explained that when an officer was in trouble for wrecking a car or something similar, other officers joked and harassed the officer involved, as a way to lighten the mood. Officer 1 explained that other officers would comfort the officer facing time off by telling the officer it is not the end of the world. Though humor is a main staple in police work, over time, officers who face adversity often become cynical. Officer 6 emphasized that officers had to distance themselves, because if they took everything personally or did not laugh about it, they would be basket cases. Officer 6 explained if officers could not handle death, they should think about a job selling insurance. Officer 6 also responded "There is nothing wrong with selling insurance, but you are probably not gonna [sic] see a lot of dead people … life is cheap and fragile, there is no rhyme or reason for death, so you either get used to it or you get out." Officer 6 noted, "If you live your life with ethics, you don't have to look over your shoulder. I try to live this way; living this way helps eliminate my stress."

Major theme 3 trust/loyalty.

Trust and loyalty are the backbone of police culture (Crank, 2004). The badge is symbolic of public trust but trust also must occur between peers and administrators.

According to Crank (2004), "It is a principal that overrides individual differences and disagreements; fealty beyond challenge" (p. 237). Fourteen of the 20 officers stated that they believed trust was apparent within their departments. Eleven of the 14 officers noted the trust that they spoke of was between peers. Of the 14 officers, only 3 officers added that they felt some degree of trust between officers and administrators. However, the 3 officers stated the trust was minimal at best.

Officer 1 stressed trust was built over time and could be lost in mere seconds. Officer 1 noted trust could be built on something as trivial as the Chief recalling a conversation about the officer's son struggling in school. Officer 1 stated that he would be utterly amazed if his Chief were to approach him several months after a conversation, and to ask him how his son was doing in school. Officer 1 concluded that trust and loyalty were built by others showing concern for your overall well-being and being genuine about the actions they display. Officer 2 explained, "The care by administration is not genuine, it is based on a liability factor." There is a belief that the care and concern displayed by those in administration is more for show and does not carry the same genuine appeal as care and concern displayed to officers by their peers. Officer 1 shared a story about the differences between care and concern displayed by peers and administrators. Officer 1 noted:

Your peers will come up and then grab your shoulders and say hey man, how are you doing? And you feel that genuine concern, maybe not to a friend level, but there's a genuine concern. When an administrator does it, and Chief walks up and grabs you by the shoulder, and says how are you doing today? He doesn't really care how you are doing today, but you are standing there and he has to ask; he has to give you that pleasantry. It's no different than saying good morning.

Part of building of trust has to do with the ways in which administrators are initially perceived by officers. Administrators must be honest and must stick to the objectives they set forth. Officer 1 explained "if he [the Chief] was open and honest and said this is what I stand for, and … then the first situation that comes up, he then sticks to the guidelines he set out." Officer 1 noted that the first conversation he had with his Chief included being told community first, department second, and officer third. When this statement was made, Officer 1 stated he felt as though he did not matter, he perceived that he was less important than the community and the department, and explained his concern in the following excerpt:

When he says it is the community first, the department second, and you third, you know when a citizen comes into complain about me, I would like for my boss to step up and go you know what, I'm gonna [sic] listen to you citizen, but in the back of his head I want him to be thinking no, this officer would not do that. You know you're not guilty until proven innocent, frequently if somebody says you're rude, you must have been rude.

Part of the frustration has to do with the way in which the law works. Criminals are innocent until proven guilty, but this does not seem to be the same criteria afforded to officers. Often, the Chief and his administration operate from the politics of City Hall and they seem to have lost the fact that they were once officers themselves. Officer 3 explained that during a staff meeting he was told if it came down to the Chief fighting for his officers or hanging his officer's out to dry, be prepared to be hung out. Officer 3 followed up this statement with "at least we knew where we stood."

Major theme 4 training.

Birzer (2003) explained that, "Police-training is an important tool in the process of facilitating change within police organizations" (p. 29). Dantzker (1999) noted that there was a lack of standardization in police training nationwide. A majority of information provided to police officers comes in the form of the sharing of *war stories* from older officers in an attempt to reinforce police culture (Kappeler, 1999). Officer 1 explained that the training provided by his department was accurate, in terms of the information provided but that the training was merely a regurgitation of what was provided in the police academy. Officer 1 noted that there was not much new information being presented and if there was new information, even being allowed to attend training was an issue of debate. Officer 1 stated the debate often involved members of the officer's union, manpower issues, and issues involving paying officers overtime to attend training.

Fourteen of the 20 officers stated that they received adequate training to perform the basic duties of the jobs. Six officers explained they had not received adequate training to perform the daily duties of the jobs. Four officers stated that they had received Critical Incident Training, which dealt briefly with issues of mental illness, depression, and suicide. However, 18 of the 20 officers interviewed emphasized they had not attended any type of training with a focus on the care and well-being of the officer. Officer 10 elaborated in the following excerpt:

The problem is that we are being trained on such a broad spectrum anymore and seems that the spectrum is being stretched further all the time … we are getting more crimes, not necessarily in number, but in terms of types of crimes. Twenty years ago, 15 years ago, no one ever thought about cyber crime and identity theft. There's a lot of competing training and because of that, there is not enough emphasis on officer well-being. These crimes take priority to the overall well-being of the officer and it is often left to the officer to try to figure it out.

Officer 11 noted that, "training can't prepare a normal thinking person for the stuff you will witness. Training can prepare you a framework but you don't even touch the surface. Nothing can compare to actually doing it." Officer 2 maintained that "we are always geared about helping everybody else but very rarely do we worry about taking care of ourselves." Douglas (2009) explained that less than 2% of all police agencies nationwide provided any type of suicide training.

Officer 4 stated that he did not know suicide was the leading cause of death for police officers. Officer 4 explained that he wished more focus was on helping law enforcement officers recover from stressful events witnessed in the line-of-duty. Officer 3 indicated that, "training is offered all the time on how to handle domestics, sex abuse cases, child sex crimes, but as far as dealing with the way these issues make you feel, or when I go home, I have never received anything for this."

Major theme 5 change.

Eighteen of the officers interviewed stated that change was taking place within their departments, whether positive or negative. The positive types of changes were indicated by 12 of the 20 officers, who believed the mindset of officers, administrators, and the community had become more accepting of mental health issues concerning law enforcement personnel. The negative types of changes were indicated by 8 of the 12 officers, who stated that they believed such changes were the result of training and increased knowledge in the areas of mental illness. Officer 20 explained officers seeking assistance outside the brotherhood were often shunned by peers. Officer 20 continued by saying that the culture "is starting to go the wayside, especially since mental health issues are on the rise." Officer 14 noted, "I think it's changed a lot in the last few years. They are making it easier for people to come forward and say I am having a problem; there is still a lot of work to do." Officer 13 stated that change was slow, in the form of department-sponsored counseling, but also noted that members of the public did not understand the struggles officers dealt with, or "just how rough the job can really be."

Knowledge facilitates change and change facilitates knowledge (Curry, Myer, & McKinney, 2006). Knowledge acquisition increases one's ability to understand and discover (Yang, 2003). One's ability to associate, reason, and learn occurs through sensation and perception (Dalkir, 2005; Shipley, Johnson, & Hashemi, 2009). Officer 8 noted that the mindset of officers was facilitating change in the culture. Officers' were being offered additional outlets to resolve issues such as divorce, PTSD, stress, and depression through Employee Assistance Programs. The mindset of the culture has become much more positive and much less judgmental on officers wishing to seek assistance for stress and depression (Officer 8).

Cultural changes in law enforcement occur at the individual and group level (Crank, 2004). Behaviorists believe that learning occurs through perception and prompts from the environment (Roy & Novotny, 2000). Cognitive theorists believe "learning has occurred if there is a change in the thought processes (unobservable), even in the absence of adjusted behavior (observable)" (Crossan et al., 1995, p. 348). Perceptions are constructed through the use of the five senses (Bush, 2006; Curry et al., 2006). Prompts from the environment influence individual perceptions and sensations, in-turn producing many unique viewpoints. Individuals belonging to a culture seek out similarities and ideas, which represent the individuals on both an individual and group level. Perception and sensation are important for learning to occur, but real change occurs when thought processes are questioned and external behaviors reflect through observable measures that such change has occurred. Crank (1997) elaborated on change by stating that until the leaders advocating change began to understand the importance of police culture on the lives of officers, limitations would exist and any effort set forth for positive change would be mute.

According to James (2003), law enforcement administrators wrestled for years with change. One of the largest changes in law enforcement has to do with the types of officers hired, as explained by Officer 2 in the following excerpt:

> It used to be to hire the meanest, biggest, strongest, 250 pounds, and you weren't gonna [sic] hired if you didn't fit this description. You had to be able to beat everybody up and go home. This is not the case anymore, it is now more touchy feely. We now focus more on the affects, (prevention).

Police officers' experiences contribute to the ever-changing role of law enforcement. "Recognizing that this role perception will change, agencies can prepare to make a positive influence on the veteran officers" (James, 2003, p. 1). The change being facilitated in law enforcement encompasses the newness and enthusiasm of young officers to the cynicism and frustration felt by veteran officers. Change is in the perceptions and mindsets of officers and encompasses the idea that change is good and should be embraced, rather than debated. James (2003) emphasized that over time veteran officers begin to resent their jobs, feeling as though they are victims of their circumstances. Veteran officers are often required to respond as leaders, even if they do not hold a title or a position within administration. Veteran officers provide influence and direction to younger officers. In-turn, veteran officers are often placed in no-win situations, which can increase resentment and stress levels.

Veteran officers may see themselves as victim management, the criminal justice system, and the community. Officers may feel that no one understands what they experience out on the street. Instead, they turn to each other to solve their problems, thereby losing the emotional support of family and friends" (James, 2003, p. 1).

Veteran officers often lack the emotional support of peers, because they are seen as leaders within the organization and are looked up to by younger officers (Crank, 204; James, 2003). According to James (2003), placing officers in a no-win situation enabled younger officers to transfer accountability to veteran officers. Veteran officers have no one to emulate or to transfer accountability to, in-turn, increasing officer stress and decreasing support systems. The lack of support systems for veteran officers should be of utmost concern to administrators, because veteran officers help shape and maintain the culture. Increasing concern for officers who lack appropriate support systems and often have increased levels of stress may result in the changing of perceptions of care and concern by administrators toward officers.

Minor theme 1 generational issues.

Officer 2 referred to the younger generation as the "thumb nation." Officer 2 stated this group of officers looked for immediate gratification. Officer 2 further stated that, "They are desensitized to fighting, but are more focused on problem-solving." The idea that "the social faux pas is no longer there in regards to being a police officer and letting your emotions show" (Officer 2).

Four of the 20 officers explained that when they were done with a shift they focused on family and tried to let the role as a police officer remain secondary until they return to work. "The younger generation may appeal for instant gratification but they seem to understand the importance of not letting the job consume them" (Officer 2). Officer 6 referred to himself as a dinosaur, because he portrayed himself as having much information to offer the younger generation. Officer 6 stated, "I have done a lot of things in my life, other than be a cop ... I see things differently than a lot of these guys, because many of these guys come straight out of college. I have life experiences." The younger generation offers insight into the technological world and this is crucial to the ever-changing profession of law enforcement.

Both generations of officers have great attributes to offer the profession of law enforcement but the generational differences should be valued. The older generation contributed to the mindset that officers must appear as strong and should not ask for assistance. According to Kureczka (1996), administrators could no longer ignore the mental health issues facing law enforcement personnel. The once non-existent issue of mental illness within the ranks of law enforcement can no longer be hidden by the generational gap. A department's lack of acknowledgement has lead to the impairment of an officer's ability to use judgment, make decisions, and perform duties (Kureczka, 1996), and can lead to civil liability against individual department's, which fail to adequately train and educate officers on the real dangers of the profession.

Minor theme 2 organizational administration.

Organizational administration, according to Crank (2004), was the number one stressor for law enforcement officers. The stress is often due to mismanagement, micro-managing, issues of trust, and segmentation, which exist between line officers and administrators (Crank, 2004; Schafer, 2008). Cultural norms for officers and administration are unique (Crank, 2004). However, it must be noted that administrators often manage through coercion (Crank, 2004). Officers are expected to make mistakes and the mistakes should in-turn be used as learning experiences (Schafer, 2008). Too often, officers are second-guessed and reprimanded for making mistakes, creating tension between officers and administrators. An officer's inability to use personal discretion can lead to increased stress (Schafer, 2008).

Officer 6 explained he had an incident where a man tried to get his gun away from him and after a brief altercation, the man then tried to go after his partner's gun, which resulted in all three men going to the ground. Officer 6 noted that, "After this incident administration called me in and chewed me out. I could see how some guys end up crying in an interview like this. I was bumming." Officer 6 went on to explain that he was doing his job and he was confident that the suspect "was not merely trying to steal his gun to pawn it." Officer 6 explained, "I did everything short of killing this guy to take him into custody and you wanna [sic] tell me how if there's smoke then there must be a fire of complaints." Officer 6 went on to explain it was not necessarily the way in which the suspect was apprehended, but the fact that race played a huge factor. Administrators feared public backlash, if this incident was made public. Officer 6 explained, "It is sensitive and it happens all over. Look, I profile. I look for criminals. I am trained to spot criminal activity or suspicious activity." Officer 6 stated that he felt like the suspect, and that it should not matter what the color of a subject's skin was, if they are breaking the law.

Officer 3 emphasized that, "It is important for your boss to establish himself as a competent cop before he tries to lead and administer, not through stories, but over time through dealing with the public and different incidents." One example given by Officer 3 involved a fatal accident, which involved numerous children. Officer 3 stated that his Chief at the time did not find the call important enough to come to the scene or to show support to the officers, "but they would not hesitate to call you at home while you were sleeping … to get all the details …that is bad administration." Officer 5 explained:

> Administration has so much to deal with that they can't begin to fathom it. They know it's bad and they don't know how to fix it. Our Chief is proactive but has met a giant stumbling stone. The mismanagement of funds in the city caused this. He would have changed things for the better, but it is gonna [sic] get bad and you can't hide that.

Officer 5 understands that there is a difference between the cultures of the line officer and administration and why there is a difference and that each group should be more cognizant of the roles and responsibilities of each group.

According to Crank (2004), "both with regard to administrative oversight and with the public, a variety of intended and unintended aspects of their occupational setting taught officers to be secretive about their behavior" (p. 277). Officers are taught early in police work, through stories and training to "lay low and avoid trouble" (Crank, 2004, p. 277). The secretive nature of line officers is a protective mechanism in place to protect officers from outsiders and administrators. Police culture has allowed the separation of powers and has allowed a dangerous level of secrecy to remain. "Legitimizing secrecy and isolation throughout the organization is a powerful way to move the police outside the realm of public accountability—loose coupling with a vengeance" (Crank, 2004, p. 278). Though it must be clear, that "as long as police conduct law enforcement under a mantle of due process and accountability in the United States, police culture will be characterized by secrecy" (Crank, 2004, p. 278).

Conclusions

Chapter 5 contained the implications of the research findings in the form of five major themes: stress, stress relief, trust/loyalty, training, and change; and two minor themes: generational issues and organizational administration. The results gained from the study may contribute to a better understanding of mental health issues, by providing officers appropriate alternatives in dealing with difficult personal situations. The contributions made in understanding mental health issues may assist officers and administrators in reducing the number of yearly officer suicides.

Police culture influences feelings, actions, and behaviors, especially during difficult circumstances (Crank, 2004; Jaramillo, Nixon, & Sams, 2005). However, training has a munificent impact on police culture. Training is a major component separating law enforcement from non-law enforcement (Kelley, 2005). Training assists officers to build skill sets such as competence, self-awareness, and self-empowerment

(Clement & Hough, 2007). Increasing officer knowledge and familiarization with topics viewed as taboo may assist with a revitalization of the culture. In the process of raising awareness, training facilitates in the reduction of prejudices and preconceived notions about unfamiliar or taboo topics (Penn & Couture, 2002).

Recommendations

The following include recommendations for the study population, law enforcement administrators, and future research. Recommendations are essential to administrators and officers in order to acknowledge the issue of law enforcement suicide. Training and educating officers and administrators on the topic of law enforcement suicide is the responsibility of all parties involved.

Recommendations for the population.

Recommendations for the population include officer and cultural acknowledgement that suicide is the number one killer of police officers' nationwide (Violanti, 2003). The singularly most powerful influence on police officer behavior is the Code of Silence (Quinn, 2005). Police culture allows officers to dictate behavior (Crank, 2004); it is therefore imperative that officers understand that police culture is no longer shielding officers from harm, but rather, mandating officers to suffer in silence. Officers can begin to reduce the stigma attached to showing emotion and talking about sensitive topics such as: stress, depression, and suicide by increasing their knowledge on these topics. According to Yang (2003), knowledge affected understanding and discovery, and knowledge changed perceptions through personal attachment to meaning in the world. Making officers aware of the issues they face in their careers will not only prepare officers personally, but may assist officers in reducing the stigma and the unknown attached to issues of mental health. Officers must open up lines of honest communication with peers and administrators if there is hope of reducing the number of yearly law enforcement suicides. Officers must prepare themselves for the physical and emotional toll law enforcement takes on the body and the mind. Dealing inappropriately (i.e., excessive drinking, drug use or abuse, domestic issues) or not dealing at all with the surmounting stress can have lasting implications of officer well-being and officer survival.

Recommendations for law enforcement leaders.

Law enforcement administrators, like officers can begin to address the problem of officer suicide by acknowledging that a problem exists and that the lack of acknowledgement has deadly consequences. A lack of acknowledgement about the issue of police suicide by administrators relays to officers that no problem exists, the problem is not concerning, or that officers who kill themselves should not have been on the force. Such denial by administrators often results in the misclassification and concealment of officer suicides, in an attempt to provide grieving families with insurance benefits and allowing departments to not have to face the shame and anger often associated with an officer suicide. Denial of an officer suicide causes department's to lose valuable governmental funding necessary to train and educate officers before suicides occur and many times training occurs as a result of an officer suicide. The lack of training and education on the topic of police suicide relays the message to officers that suicide is not a problem and those entrusted to take care of them do not feel the mental health and overall well-being of the officer is vitally important.

Many times the lack of acknowledgement about officer suicide is merely a coping mechanism used to protect officers and family members from the taboo nature of the act. If a suicide occurs, officers must be allowed appropriate time to grieve and officers should be allowed the opportunity to attend funeral, to display mourning bands, use departmental vehicles in the funeral procession, and to be able to speak to a counselor or a professional about the situation if they choose. Administrators who deny a suicide has occurred or those who do not allow an appropriate time to grieve the loss of an officer run the risk of dealing with officers who feel as though the life of a fellow officer was trivialized, and over time, officers begin to resent administration. Officers should be allowed to grieve in the way that best allows them to deal with the pain and hurt they may be experiencing.

Law enforcement administrators must understand the importance of changing officer perceptions about the stigma attached to issues dealing with mental health, by helping to break down barriers which exist within the culture (Overton & Medina, 2008; Violanti, Castellano, O'Rourke, & Paton, 2006). Administrators should work diligently in reducing the stigma attached to such things as: depression, mental illness, stress, and suicide. Police work is a high stress job. Accumulating stress takes a toll on the body, mind, and psyche. Administrators themselves should remember that they too were once officers and to remember the stress they faced. Administrators can begin to relate to their officers more by opening up the lines of communication, while providing adequate outlets for officers to feel safe enough to seek assistance for issues concerning their mental health. Administrators must allow officers the necessary and appropriate time to grieve after an officer suicide

Recommendations for future research.

There are six recommendations for future research. The first recommendation is to conduct a replication of the study in different geographical areas within the United States, as suicide rates fluctuate in different geographical areas (Jamison, 1999). According to the WHO (2006), over 1 million people commit suicide worldwide every year (para. 1). Suicide is an act, which does not discriminate. People of all sexes, ages, ethnicities, and occupations have died by their own hand. Suicide in all age groups (i.e., 18 – 65 years of age) in the United States is the ninth leading cause of death (CDC, 2005); resulting in approximately 30,000 people taking their own lives each year (NCHS, 2005, para. 1). Western states account for increased rates of suicide ("Facts and figures," 2009); whereas states located in the North and East have lower incidence of suicide ("Facts and figures," 2009).

The second recommendation is to conduct a study of White, female law enforcement officers. White, males' account for the largest number of completed suicides annually in the United States, but White, females have a higher incidence of suicide attempts compared to their male counter parts (CDC, 2005). With an increasing number of females in law enforcement positions, it is necessary to discuss the changing dynamic. In an attempt to bond with male counterparts, female officers may view suicide as a more viable option. The Code of Silence, which shields officers, is no longer protecting them from the devastation of suicide. Modifications must be made within the individual and within the group thought processes. Cognitive learning theory allows for modifications in thought processes, in which through mutual understanding and shared value systems, change is revealed (Crossan et al., 1995; Roy & Novotny, 2000).

The third recommendation is to conduct a quantitative study relating to officer perceptions of care. Perception is driven by the sensation of the five senses. Perception is one's ability to accept the sensory inputs and through a thought process is able to filter what appears to be relevant (Curry et al., 2006). Perception can also be flawed within individuals and within groups. Groups who have flawed perceptions and thought processes are constantly reaffirming beliefs within the individuals in the group. The ability for an individual to change group perceptions is often difficult. An officer suffering from mental illness may not be able to articulate accurate perceptions of care by peers, so it remains imperative that the culture break down the walls of silence and implement positive thought patterns about mental illness, while reducing the stigma attached to issues of mental health.

Qualitative studies can be easily conducted and can adapt to a larger sample size. A qualitative study may also reduce officer hesitancy about openly discussing the topic of police suicide. The fourth recommendation is to conduct a study to include perceptions of care given to officers and training's impact on the issue of officer suicide by law enforcement administration and key stakeholders. The results of the study may benefit current and future law enforcement administrators who may encounter officers dealing with difficult situations or officers exhibiting the signs and symptoms of depression and mental illness. Law enforcement administrators must understand the importance of changing officer perceptions about stigma attached to issues of mental health, by helping break down barriers in law enforcement culture (Overton & Medina, 2008; Violanti, Castellano, O'Rourke, & Paton, 2006).

The fifth recommendation is to conduct a study of officers who have been subject to variations of emotional dysregulation, as a response to abuse (i.e., verbal physical, and emotional) during childhood (i.e., up to 18 years of age). According to Putnam and Silk (2005), emotional dysregulation was defined as a variation in moods and behaviors, which were classified as outside the norm. The risk of suicide increases in individuals suffering from emotional dysregulation, especially if the abuse occurred early in childhood. Human learning occurs through prompts from the environment (Roy & Novotny, 2000). Suicidal behaviors have been linked to factors within the environment. Individuals experiencing numerous degrees of emotional dysregulation also have difficulty relaying the information for others to understand their experiences.

Oftentimes, individuals will hide the suffering and abuse. The inability of individuals to share such information leaves them feeling like outsiders in society and may also cause a disconnection within the police culture. Law enforcement officers often experience high levels of stress and trauma due to the nature of police work (Crank, 2004). Traumatic events may trigger increased dysfunctional thoughts and behaviors in individuals suffering from emotional dysregulation, causing individuals to lose basic problem-solving skills (Putnam & Silk, 2005). The increased risk of suicide often occurs when problem-solving skills are minimized and dysfunctional thought patterns appear, leaving those individuals who suffer to believe few options exist other than suicide (Putnam & Silk, 2005).

The sixth recommendation is to work on establishing accurate documenting procedures for law enforcement suicides. The debate remains that law enforcement suicides occur at the rate of 140 to 500 per year. Either way, suicide is either the number one or number two killer of law enforcement personnel. Currently, there are no government agencies, which capture, accurately, the number of yearly law enforcement suicides. In order for funding to be distributed for training and education on the topic, accurate numbers must be recorded. In order for accurate numbers to be recorded, the stigma attached to suicide and issues dealing with mental illness must be reduced. According to Ramos (2010), if such an agency existed, "it would end the debate on how serious this problem really is" (personal communication, February 09, 2010).

Concluding Remarks

Suicide is a public health concern of epidemic proportions (CDC, 2005; Satcher, 1999). Suicide claims approximately 1 million lives worldwide annually (WHO, 2006, p. 2). Suicide rates increase within occupations exposed to stress and trauma, such as law enforcement (Violanti et al., 2007; Waters & Ussery, 2007). In fact, suicide is the leading cause of death for law enforcement officers nationwide (PSF, 2008a). Law enforcement suicide is a taboo topic that many would rather sweep under the rug, but it must be noted that suicide is preventable. The loss of life is tragic, but what remain more tragic remain the lack of acknowledgment by administrators and officers about this epidemic, a lack of training and education on the topic of police suicide, and the lack of accurate reporting procedures, which could end the debate about the seriousness of police suicide. Perceptions about mental health issues must be addressed in order to begin changing the culture.

References

Aamodt, M. G., & Stalnaker, N. A. (2001). Police officer suicide: Frequency and officer profile. In D.C. Sheehan & J. I. Warren (Eds.), *Suicide and law enforcement* (pp. 383-398). Quantico, VA: U.S. Department of Justice.

American Foundation for Suicide Prevention. (2009). Facts and figures: State statistics. Retrieved August 07, 2009, from http://www.afsp.org/index.cfm?fuseaction= home.viewpage&page_id=05114FBE-E445-7831-F0C1494E2FADB8EA

American Psychological Association. (2009). *APA government relations: Science policy.* Retrieved April 27, 2009, from www.apa.org/ppo/science/

Andrew, L. B. (2008). *Physician suicide*. Retrieved February 25, 2009, from http://emedicine.medscape.com/article/806779-overview

Arboleda-Florez, J., & Sartorius, N. (2008). *Understanding stigma of mental illness: Theory and intervention.* Hoboken, NJ: John Wiley & Sons.

Baddeley, A. D. (2004). *Your memory: A user's guide.* Buffalo, NY: Firefly Books.

Baker, M. (1985). *Cops: Their lives in their own words.* New York, NY: Pocket Books.

Barnett, J. E., Johnson-Greene, D., Wise, E. H., & Bucky, S. F. (2007). Informed consent: Too much of a good thing or not enough? *Professional Psychology: Research and Practice, 38*(2), 179-186.

Bertolote, J. M., Fleischmann, A., De Leo, D., & Wasserman, D. (2004). Psychiatric diagnoses and suicide: Revisiting the evidence. *Crisis, 25*(4), 147-155.

Birzer, M. L. (2003). The theory of andragogy applied to police training. *Policing: An International Journal of Police Strategies & Management, 25*(1), 29-42.

Black, D. (1980). *Manners and customs of the police.* New York, NY: Academic Press.

Blackmore, J. (1978). Are police allowed to have problems of their own? *Police Magazine, 1*(3), 47-54.

Blum, L. N. (2000). *Force under pressure: How cops live and why they die.* New York, NY: Lantern Books.

Boeree, C. G. (2006). *Personality theories: Sigmund Freud.* Retrieved May 05, 2008, from http://www.ship.edu/~cgboeree/freud.html

Boyd, C. O. (2001). Phenomenology the method. In P. L. Munhall (Ed.), *Nursing research: A qualitative perspectives* (3rd ed.) (pp. 93-122). Sudbury, MA: Jones & Bartlett.

Brown, M. K. (1988). *Working the street: Police discretion and the dilemmas of reform.* New York, NY: Russell Sage Foundation.

Brown, M. Z. (2006). Linehan's theory of suicidal behavior: Theory, research and dialectical behavior therapy. In T.E.Ellis (2006), *Cognition and suicide: Theory, research, and therapy* (pp. 91-117). Washington, DC: American Psychological Association.

Bureau of Justice Statistics. (2009). *State and local law enforcement statistics.* Washington, DC: Author.

Burke, R. J., & Mikkelsen, A. (2007). Suicidal ideation among police officers in Norway. *Policing: An International Journal of Police Strategies & Management, 30*(2), 228-236.

Bush, G. (2006). Learning about learning: From theories to trends. *Teacher Librarian, 34*(2), 14.

Cancino, J. M., & Enriquez, R. (2004). A qualitative analysis of police peer retaliation: Preserving the police culture. *Policing: An International Journal of Police Strategies & Management, 27*(3), 320-340.

Carter, D. L. (1985). Police brutality: A model for definition, perspective, and control. In A. S. Blumberg, & E. Niederhoffer (Eds.), *The ambivalent force* (pp. 148-156). New York, NY: Holt, Rinehart, and Winston.

Center for Disease Control and Prevention. (2005). *Suicide: Facts at a glance.* Retrieved May 06, 2008, from www.cdc.gov/ncipc/dvp/suicide/SuicideDataSheet.pdf

Chamberlain, C. (2000). *Violence and mental illness: Mentally ill attack at a higher rate.* Retrieved April 05, 2009, from http://www.namiscc.org/newsletters/April02/Violence.htm

Christos, G. (2003). *Memory and dreams: The creative human mind.* New Brunswick, NJ: Rutgers University Press.

Clark, D. W., & White, E. K. (2003). Clinicians, cops, and suicide. In D. P. Hackett, & J. M. Violanti (Eds.), *Police suicide: Tactics for prevention* (pp. 16-36). Springfield, IL: Charles C. Thomas.

Clement, K., Hough, R. M., & Jones, B. (2007). Partnering with a purpose. *The Police Chief, 74*(11).

Cooper, V. G., McLearen, A. M., & Zapf, P. A. (2004). Dispositional decisions with the mentally ill: Police perceptions and characteristics. *Police Quarterly, 7,* 295-310.

Crank, J. P. (2004). *Understanding police culture* (2nd ed.). Cincinnati, OH: Anderson Publishing.

Creswell, J. W. (2005). *Educational research: Planning, conducting, and evaluating quantitative and qualitative research* (2nd ed.). Upper Saddle River, NJ: Prentice-Hall.

Creswell, J. W. (2009). *Research design: Qualitative, quantitative, and mixed methods approaches* (3rd ed.). Thousand Oaks, CA: Sage Publications.

Cross, C. L., & Ashley, L. (2004). Police trauma and addiction: Coping with dangers on the job. *FBI Law Enforcement Bulletin, 73*(10), 24-32.

Crossan, M. M., Lane, H. W., White, R. E., & Djurfeldt, L. (1995). Organizational learning: Dimensions for a theory. *The International Journal of Organizational Analysis, 3*(4), 337-360.

Crowder, R. G. (1976). *Principles of learning and memory.* Hillsdale, NJ: John Wiley & Sons.

Curry, D. G., Meyer, J. E., & McKinney, J. M. (2006). *Seeing versus perceiving: What you see isn't always what you get.* Des Plaines, IL: Professional Safety.

Dalkir, K. (2005). *Knowledge management in theory and practice.* Burlington, MA: Elsevier, Inc.

Department of Mental Health. (2006). *Erasing the stigma of mental illness.* Retrieved March 23, 2009, from http:www.state.sc.us/dmh/erasing_stigma.htm

De Paulo, J. R., & Horvitz, L. A. (2002). *Understanding depression: What we know and what you can do about it.* Hoboken, NJ: John Wiley & Sons.

Diamond, D. (2003). Departmental barriers to mental health treatment: A precursor to police officer suicide. In D. P. Hackett & J. M. Violanti. *Police suicide: Tactics for prevention* (pp. 54-65). Springfield, IL: Charles C. Thomas.

Diggory, J. C. (1976). The components of personal despair. In E. S. Schneidman (Ed.), *Essays in self-destruction* (pp. 300-321). New York, NY: Science House, Inc.

Douglas, R, (1997). *Death with no valor.* Pasadena, MD: Keener Marketing Inc.

Durkheim, E. (1979). *Suicide: A study in sociology.* New York, NY: The Free Press.

Edmondson, A. C., Winslow, A. B., Bohmer, R. M. J., & Pisan, G. P. (2002). Different patterns of performance improvement for tacit and explicit knowledge: An empirical test. *Academy of Management Proceedings*, B1-B6.

Evans, R. & Crank, J. (2004). The culture eater. In J. P. Crank (2003). *Understanding police culture* (pp. 339-352). Boca Raton, FL: Anderson Publishing.

Falk, G. (2001). *STIGMA: How we treat outsiders*. Amherst, NY: Prometheus Books.

Fendrich, M., Kruesi, M. J. P., Grossman, J., Wislar, J. S., & Freeman, K. (1998). Police collection of firearms to prevent suicide: Correlates of recent turn-in experience. *Policing: An International Journal of Police Strategies & Management, 21*(1), 8-21.

Fiol, C. M., & Lyles, M. A. (1985). Organizational learning. *Academy of Management Review, 10*, 803-813.

Franzoi, S. L. (2005). *Social psychology* (4th ed.). Boston, MA: McGraw-Hill.

Frey, A. (2007). *Blue wall of silence perceived in police force*. Retrieved December 05, 2007, from www.dailybulletin.com/news/ci_3503381

Freud, E. (1935). *The origin and development of psychoanalysis*. Chicago, IL: Henry Regnery Company.

Glaser, B. G., & Strauss, A. L. (1999). *The discovery of grounded theory: Strategies for qualitative research.* New York, NY: Aldine De Gruyter.

Good, T. L., & Brophy, J. E. (1990). *Educational psychology: A realistic approach* (4th ed.). White Plains, NY: Longman.

Gray, M.J., & Lombardo, T.W. (2004, January/March). Life event attributions as a potential source of vulnerability following exposure to a traumatic event. *Journal of Loss & Trauma, 9*(1), 59-72.

Hackett, D. P., & Violanti, J. M. (2003). *Police suicide: Tactics for prevention.* Springfield, IL: Charles C. Thomas.

Hackett, D. P. (2003). Suicide and the police. In D. P. Hackett & J. M. Violanti (Eds.), *Police suicide: Tactics for prevention* (pp. 7-15). Springfield, IL Charles C. Thomas.

Hall, R. G. (2002). *A brief discussion of police culture and how it affects police response to internal investigations and civilian oversight.* Retrieved February 14, 2009, from http://www.cacole.ca/Resource%20Library/Conferences/2002 %20Conference/2002%20Presentations/Hall,%20R.%202002.pdf

Harrison, S. J. (1998). *Police organizational culture: Using ingrained values to build positive organizational improvement.* Retrieved September 23, 2008, from http://www.pamij.com/harrison.html

Hassell, K.D. (2006). *Police organizational cultures and patrol practices.* New York, NY: LFB Scholarly Publishing.

He, N., Zhao, J., & Archbold, C. A. (2002). Gender and police stress: The convergent and divergent impact of work environment, work-family conflict, and stress coping mechanisms of female and male police officers. *Policing: An International Journal of Police Strategies & Management, 25*(4), 687-708.

Heim, C., Nater, U. M., Maloney, E., Boneva, R., Jones, J. F., & Reeves, W. C. (2009). Childhood trauma and risk for chronic fatigue syndrome: Association with neuroendocrine dysfunction. *Archives of General Psychiatry, 66*(1), 72-80.

Henry, V. E. (1995). The police officer as survivor: Death confrontations and the police subculture. *Behavioral Science and Law, 11*(1), 93-112.

Henry, V. E. (2004). *Death work: Police, trauma, and the psychology of survival.* New York, NY: Oxford University Press.

Hicks, R. C., Dattero, R., & Gallup, S. D. (2007). A metaphor for knowledge management: Explicit islands in a tacit sea. *Journal of Knowledge Management, 11*(1), 5-17.

Horne, P. (2006). Policewomen: Their 1st century and the new era. *The Police Chief, 73*(9).

Jamison, K. R. (1999). *Night falls fast: Understanding suicide.* New York, NY: Random House.

Janata, P. (2008). *What is the connection between stress and depression?* Retrieved September 29, 2008, from http://abcnews.go.com/Health/StressOverview/ story?id=4672875

Jaramillo, F., Nixon, R., & Sams, D. (2005). The effect of law enforcement stress on organizational commitment. *Policing: An International Journal of Police Strategies & Management, 28*(2), 321-336.

Jiao, A. Y. (2001). Police and culture: A comparison between China and the United States. *Police Quarterly, 4*(2), 156-185.

Joiner, T. (2005). *Why people die by suicide.* Cambridge, MA: Harvard University Press.

Jung, C. G. (1923). *Psychological types*. London, UK: Routledge & Kegan Paul.

Kappeler, V. E. (1999). *The police and society* (2nd ed.). Prospect Heights, IL: Waveland Press, Inc.

Kappeler, V. E., Sluder, R. D., & Alpert, G. P. (1998). *Forces of deviance: Understanding the dark side of policing* (2nd ed.). Prospect Heights, IL: Waveland Press, Inc.

Karlsson, I., & Christianson, S.A. (2003). The phenomenology of traumatic experiences in police work. *Policing: An International Journal of Police Strategies & Management, 26*(3), 419-438.

Kates, A. R. (1999). *Cop shock: Surviving posttraumatic stress disorder (PTSD)*. Tucson, AZ: Holbrook Street Press.

Kates, A. R. (2008). *PTSD: The secret cop killer*. Retrieved December 03, 2008, from http://www.calea.org/Online/newsletter/No87/ptsd.htm

Kelley, T. M. (2005). Mental health and prospective police professionals. *Policing: An International Journal of Police Strategies & Management, 28*(1), 6-29.

Kelly, P., & Martin, R. (2006). Police suicide is real. *Law & Order, 54*(3), 93-95.

Kirk, J., & Miller, M. L. (1986). *Reliability and validity in qualitative research*. Beverly Hills, CA: Sage Publications.

Kirschman, E. (2007). *I love a cop: What police families need to know* (Rev. ed.). New York, NY: The Guilford Press.

Klein, D.F., & Wender, P.H. (2005). *Understanding depression: A complete guide to its diagnosis and treatment*. New York, NY: Oxford University Press.

Klingberg, T. (2009). *The overflowing brain: Information overload and the limits of the working memory.* New York, NY: Oxford University Press.

Kottler, P. & Keller, K. L. (2006). *Marketing management.* Upper Saddle River: NJ: Pearson-Prentice Hall.

Kroes, W. H. (1976). *Society's victim-the policeman: An analysis of the job stress in policing.* Springfield, IL: Charles C. Thomas.

Kuhn, T. S. (1996). *The structure of scientific revolutions* (3rd ed.). Chicago, IL: The University of Chicago Press.

Kureczka, A. W. (1996). Critical incident stress in law enforcement. *FBI Law Enforcement Bulletin, 65*(2/3), 10-16.

Lejoyeux, M., Huet, F., Claudon, M., Fichelle, A., Casalino, E., & Lequen, V. (2008). Characteristics of suicide attempts preceded by alcohol consumption. *Archives of Suicide Research, 12*(1), 30-38.

Liberman, A. M., Best, S. R., Metzler, T. J., Weiss, D. S., & Marmar, C. R. (2002). Routine occupational stress and psychological distress in police. *Policing: An International Journal of Police Strategies & Management, 25*(2), 421-439.

Lindsay, V. (2008). Police officers and their alcohol consumption: Should we be concerned? *Police Quarterly, 11*(1), 74-87.

Lindsay, V., Taylor, W.B., & Shelley, K. (2008). Alcohol and the police: An empirical examination of widely-held assumption. *Policing: An International Journal of Police Strategies & Management, 31*(4), 596-609.

Linehan, M. M. (1986). Suicidal people: One population or two? *Annals of the New York Academy of Sciences, 487,* 16-33.

Linehan, M. M. (1993). *Cognitive-behavioral treatment of borderline personality disorder.* New York, NY: Guilford Press.

Linehan, M. M. (1995). *Understanding borderline personality disorder: The dialectics approach program manual.* New York, NY: Guilford Press.

Loo, R. (2004). A typology of burnout types among police managers. *Policing: An International Journal of Police Strategies & Management, 27*(2), 156-165.

Marcus, E. (1996). *Why suicide?* New York, NY: Harper Collins Publisher.

Maslach, C. (1976). Burnout. *Human Behavior, 23*, 16-22.

Maslow, A. H. (1943). A theory of human motivation. *Psychological Review, 50*, 370-96.

Maxfield, M. G., & Babbie, E. (2005). *Research methods for criminal justice and criminology* (4th ed.). Belmont, CA: Sage Publications.

Mental Health America. (2009). *Factsheet: Stigma: Building awareness and understanding.* Retrieved March 23, 2009, from http://www.mentalhealthamerica.net/go/action/stigma-watch

Misdiagnosis of depression. (2009). Retrieved July 04, 2009, from http://www.wrongdiagnosis.com/d/depression/misdiag.htm

Mitchell, J. T., & Everly, G. S. (1993). *Critical incident stress debriefing: An operations manual for the prevention of traumatic stress among emergency services and disaster workers.* Ellicott City, MD: Chevron.

Miyazaki, A., & Taylor, K. (2008). Researcher interaction biases and business ethics research: Respondent reactions to research characteristics. *Journal of Business Ethics, 81*(4), 779-795.

Monaghan, J., & Just, P. (2000). *Social & cultural anthropology: A very short introduction.* New York, NY: Oxford University Press.

Morash, M., Haarr, R., & Kwak, D. H. (2006). Multilevel influences on police stress. *Journal of Contemporary Criminal Justice, 22*(1), 26-43.

Moustakas, C. (1994). *Phenomenological research methods.* Thousand Oaks, CA: Sage Publications.

Mullins, W. C. (2001). The relationship between police officer suicide and posttraumatic stress disorder. In D. C. Sheehan and J. I. Warren (Eds.), *Suicide and law enforcement* (pp. 257-265). Washington DC: U.S. Department of Justice.

Nagourney, E. (2007, April 17). *At risk: Availability of guns raises suicide rates, study finds.* Retrieved June 16, 2007, from http://www.nytimes.com/2007/04/17/health/17risk.html

National Center for Health Statistics. (2005). *Suicide and self-inflicted injury.* Retrieved May 07, 2008, from http://www.cdc.gov/nchs/fastats/suicide.htm

National Institute of Mental Health. (2004). *Depression: A treatable illness (fact sheet).* Retrieved June 08, 2009, from http://www.nimh.nih.gov/health/publications/depression-a-treatable-illness-fact-sheet/index.shtml

National Institute of Mental Health. (2009). *The numbers count: Mental disorders in America.* Bethesda, MD: Author.

National Police Suicide Foundation. (2008a). *Introduction: Understanding the problem is key.* Baltimore, MD: Author.

National Police Suicide Foundation. (2008b). *Post-traumatic stress disorder.* Baltimore, MD: Author.

National Police Suicide Foundation. (2008c). *Warning signs of police burnout.*
Baltimore, MD: Author.

Neuman, W. L. (2005). *Social research methods: Qualitative and quantitative approaches* (6th ed.). Boston, MA: Allyn and Bacon.

Ngwenyama, O. (2001). *Doing phenomenological research.* Retrieved April 22, 2009, from http://www.cs.aau.dk/~pan/phd-doc/Phenomenological-Research.ppt

Niederhoffer, A. (1967). *Behind the shield: The police in urban society.* Garden City, NY: Anchor Books.

Nonaka, I. & Nishiguchi, T. (2001). *Knowledge emergence: Social, technical, and evolutionary dimensions of knowledge creation.* New York, NY: Oxford University Press.

Officer Down Memorial Page, Inc. (2004). *Honoring officers killed in the year 2004.* Retrieved May 15, 2009, from http://www.odmp.org/year.php?year= 2004&Submit=Go

Officer Down Memorial Page, Inc. (2005). *Honoring officers killed in the year 2005.* Retrieved May 15, 2009, from http://www.odmp.org/year.php.year?= 2005&Submit=Go

Officer Down Memorial Page, Inc. (2006). *Honoring officers killed in the year 2006.* Retrieved May 15, 2009, from http://www.odmp.org/year.php?year= 2006&Submit=Go

Officer Down Memorial Page, Inc. (2007). *Honoring officers killed in the year 2007.* Retrieved May 15, 2009, from http://www.odmp.org/year.php?year= 2007&Submit=Go

Officer Down Memorial Page, Inc. (2008). *Honoring officers killed in 2008.* Retrieved

    May 15, 2009, from http://www.odmp.org/year.php?year=2008&Submit=Go

Officer Down Memorial Page, Inc. (2009). *Honoring officers killed in 2009.* Retrieved

    May 15, 2009, from http://www.odmp.org/year.php

O'Hara, A. (2009). *Police suicide numbers and the chicken little factor.* Retrieved

    January 27, 2010, from http://www.policesuicidestudy.com/id4.htm

O'Hara, A. F., & Violanti, J. M. (2009). Police suicide: A web surveillance of national

    data. *International Journal of Emergency Mental Health, 11*(1), 17-24.

Ott, E. E. (1996). *The nature of knowledge.* Retrieved March 09, 2009, from

    http://www.futureperspective.com/know.htm

Overton, S. L., & Medina, S. L. (2008). The stigma of mental illness. *Journal of*

    Counseling & Development, 86(2), 143-151.

Patton, M. Q. (1990). *Qualitative evaluation and research methods* (2nd ed.). Thousand

    Oaks, CA: Sage Publications.

Pegula, S. M. (2004). *An analysis of workplace suicides, 1992-2001.* Washington, DC:

    U.S. Bureau of Labor Statistics.

Penn, D. L., & Couture, S. M. (2002). Strategies for reducing stigma toward persons with

    mental illness. *World Psychiatry, 1*(1), 20-21.

Perin, M. (2007). Police suicide. *Law Enforcement Technology, 34*(9), 8.

Piner, K. E., & Kahle, L. R. (1984). Adapting to the stigmatizing label of mental illness:

    Foregone but not forgotten. *Journal of Personality and Social Psychology, 47,*

    805-11.

Polisar, J., & Milgram, D. (1998). Recruiting, integrating, and retaining women police officers: Strategies that work. *The Police Chief Magazine, 65*(10), 42-52.

Putnam, K. M., & Silk, K. R. (2005). Emotion dysregulation and the development of borderline personality disorder. *Development and Psychopathology, 17*(4), 899-925.

QSR International. (2007). *Products: Nvivo8.* Retrieved June 28, 2009, from http://www.qsrinternational.com/products_nvivo.aspx

QSR International. (2008). *NVivo8: Getting started.* Retrieved June 26, 2009, from http://www.qsrinternational.com/FileResourceHandler.ashx/RelatedDocuments/DocumentFile/289/NVivo8-Getting-Started-Guide.pdf

Quinn, M. W. (2005). *Walking with the devil: The police code of silence.* Minneapolis, MN: Quinn and Associates.

Raffel-Price, B. (1996). Female police officers in the U. S. Retrieved August 05, 2009, from http://www.ncjrs.gov/policing/fem635.htm

Ratey, J. J. (2002). *A user's guide to the brain: Perception, attention, and the four theaters of the brain.* New York, NY: Vintage Books.

Reiner, R. (1978). *The blue-coated worker: A sociological study of police unionism.* New York, NY: Cambridge University Press.

Reiss, A., Jr. (1971). *Police and the public.* New Haven, CT: Yale University Press.

Ross, D. L. (2000). Emerging trends in police failure to train liability. *Policing: An International Journal of Police Strategies & Management, 23*(2), 169-193.

Roy, L., & Novotny, E. (2000). How do we learn? Contributions of learning theory to reference service and library instruction. *The Reference Librarian, 69/70*, 129-139.

Rudofossi, D.C. (2007). *Working with traumatized police-officer patients: A clinician's guide to complex PTSD syndromes in public safety professionals (Death, value, and meaning).* Amityville, NY: Baywood Publishing Co.

Saari, S., & Silver, A. (2005). *A bolt from the blue: Coping with disasters and acute traumas* (2nd ed.). Philadelphia, PA: Athenaeum Press.

Sage, G. H. (1984). *Motor learning and control: A neuropsychological approach.* Dubuque, IA: Wm. C. Brown Publishers.

Sales, B. D., & Kahle, L. R. (1980). Law and attitudes toward the mentally ill. *International Journal of Law & Psychiatry, 3*, 391-403.

Satcher, D. (1999). *The surgeon general's call to action to prevent suicide 1999.* Washington, DC: United States Public Health Service.

Schafer, J. A. (2008). Effective police leadership: Experiences and perspectives of law enforcement leaders. *The FBI Law Enforcement Bulletin, 77*(7), 13-19.

Scott, E. (2005). Managing municipal police training programs with limited resources. *The Police Chief, 72*(10), 1-3).

Seidel, J. V. (1998). *Qualitative data analysis.* Retrieved March 13, 2009, from http://www.scribd.com/doc/7129360/Seidel-1998-Qualitative-Data-Analysis

Shneidman, E. S. (1985). *Definition of suicide.* New York, NY: Wiley & Sons.

Shneidman, E. S. (1996). *The suicidal mind.* New York, NY: Oxford University Press.

Shneidman, E. S., & Farberow, N. L. (1957). The logic of suicide. In E.S. Schneidman,

    N. L. Farberow and R. E. Litman (1995), *The psychology of suicide* (pp. 63-71).

    New York, NY: Jason Aronson, Inc.

Shneidman, E. S., & Mandelkorn, P. (1983). How to prevent suicide. In E. S.

    Shneidman, N. L. Farberow, & R. E. Litman (Eds.), *The psychology of suicide*

    (pp. 125-143). New York, NY: Jason Aronson, Inc.

Shipley, M. F., Johnson, M., & Hashemi, S. (2009). Cognitive learning style and its

    effects on the perception of learning, satisfaction and social interactions in virtual

    teams. *The Journal of American Academy of Business, 14*(2), 17-27.

Silverman, D. (2004). *Qualitative research: Theory, method and practice* (2nd ed.).

    Thousand Oaks, CA: Sage Publications.

Sipkoff, M. (2006). Depression in the workplace costs employers billions per year:

    Employers take lead in fighting depression. *Managed Care Magazine, 1*(1), 1-22.

Sokolowski, R. (2007). *Introduction to phenomenology.* Cambridge University Press.

Strauss, A. & Corbin, J. (1990). *Basics of qualitative research: Grounded theory*

    procedures and techniques. Newbury Park, CA: Sage Publications.

Stevens, M. (2005). *Police culture and behavior.* Retrieved January 04, 2008, from

    http://faculty.ncwc.edu/mstevens/205/205lect02.htm

Suicide on the force, Code of silence doesn't help. (1997). Retrieved June 17, 2007, from

    http://www.psf.org/media.htm

Tate, T. (2004). *Police suicide-What can be done?* Retrieved November 30, 2007, from

    http://www.tearsofacop.com/police/articles/tate.html

Terry, S. (2009). *Learning and memory: Basic principles, processes, and procedures* (4th ed.). Washington, DC: Pearson Education, Inc.

Trautman, N. (2001). *The truth about police code of silence revealed.* Retrieved April 03, 2009, from http://www.ethicsinstitute.com/pdf/Code%20of%20Silence %20Facts%20Revealed.pdf

Treating depression: Is effective treatment available. (2009). *CQ Researcher, 19*(24), 573-596.

Triandis, H., (1994). *Culture and social behavior.* New York, NY: McGraw-Hill.

Tuck, I. (2009). On the edge: Integrating spirituality into law enforcement. *FBI Law Enforcement Bulletin, 78*(5), 14-21.

United States Public Health Service. (1999). *The surgeon general's call to action to prevent suicide.* Washington, DC: Author.

United States Public Health Service. (n.d.). *Mental health: A report of the surgeon general.* Retrieved January 05, 2009, from http://www.surgeongeneral.gov/ library/mentalhealth/home.html

Ursano, R. J., & McCarroll, J. E. (1990). The nature of traumatic stressor: handling dead bodies. *The Journal of Nervous & Mental Disease, 178*(6), 396-398.

van Manen, M. (1990). *Researching the lived experience: Human science for an action sensitive pedagogy.* Albany, NY: State University of New York Press.

van Praag, H. M. (2004). Stress and suicide are we well-equipped to study this issue? *The Journal of Crisis Intervention & Suicide Prevention, 25*(2), 80-85.

Violanti, J. M. (1995). The mystery within: Understanding police suicide. *The FBI Law Enforcement Bulletin, 4,* 19-23.

Violanti, J. M. (1996). *Police suicide: Epidemic in blue.* Springfield, IL: Charles C. Thomas.

Violanti, J. M. (2003). Suicide and the police culture. In D. P. Hackett & J. M. Violanti (Eds.), *Police suicide: Tactics for prevention* (pp. 66-75). Springfield, IL; Charles C. Thomas.

Violanti, J. M. (2005). Dying for the job: Psychological stress, disease, and morality in police work. In H. Copes (2004), *Policing and stress* (pp. 87-102). Upper Saddle River, NJ: Pearson Prentice-Hall.

Violanti, J. M. (2007). *Police suicide: Epidemic in blue* (2nd ed.). Springfield, IL: Charles C. Thomas.

Violanti, J. M., & Aron, F. (1994). Ranking police stressors. *Psychological Reports, 75*, 824.

Violanti, J. M., Castellano, C., O'Rourke, J., & Paton, D. (2006). Proximity to the 9/11 terrorist attack and suicide ideation in police officers. *Traumatology, 12*(3), 248-254.

Violanti. J. M., Fekedulegn, D., Charles, L. E., Andrew, M. E., Hartley, T. A., Mnatsakanova, A. et al. (2008). Suicide in police work: Exploring potential contributing factors. *American Journal of Criminal Justice, 34*(1), 41.

Violanti, J. M., & Samuels, S. (2007). *Under the blue shadow: Clinical and behavioral perspectives on policed suicide.* Springfield, IL: Charles C. Thomas.

Violanti, J. M. (2008). Police suicide research: Conflict and consensus. *International Journal of Emergency Mental Health, 10*(4), 299-308.

Violanti, J. M., Fekedulegn, D., Charles, L. E., Andrew, M. E., Hartley, T. A., Mnatsakanova, A., et al. (2008). Suicide in police work: Exploring potential contributing influences. *American Journal of Criminal Justice, 34*(1), 41.

Waters, J. A., & Ussery, W. (2007). Police stress: history, contributing factors, symptoms, and interventions. *Policing: An International Journal of Police Strategies & Management, 30*(2), 168-188

Weisinger, H. (1985). *The anger workout book.* New York, NY: Quill.

Wells, W. M., & Schafer, J. A. (2006). Officer perceptions of police responses to persons with a mental illness: Evidence from five departments in Indiana. *Policing: An International Journal of Police Strategies and Management, 29*, 578-601.

Woody, R. H. (2005). The police culture: Research implications for psychological services. *Professional Psychology: Research and Practice, 36*(5), 535-529.

World Health Organization. (2000). *Preventing suicide: A resource for media professionals.* Geneva, Switzerland: Department of Mental Health.

World Health Organization. (2006). *Suicide prevention.* Geneva, Switzerland: Department of Public Health.

World Health Organization. (2009). *Mental health.* Retrieved March 23, 2009, from http://www.who.int/mental_health/en/

Worrall, J. L. (2001). The reasonably unreasonable officer: A paradox in police civil liability jurisprudence. *Policing: An International Journal of Police Strategies & Management, 24*(4), 449-469.

Yang, B. (2003). Toward a holistic theory of knowledge and adult learning. *Human Resource Development Review, 2*(2), 106-129.

Yin, R. K. (2009). *Case study research: Design and Methods* (5nd ed.). Thousand Oaks,

CA: Sage.

APPENDIX A: CONTEXTUAL, STRUCTURAL, AND HUMAN CONDITIONS

Contextual, Structural, and Human Conditions

Conditions	Perception	Learning	Behavior
Contextual	Cultural diversity (Jiao, 2001) Shared Values and Beliefs (Brown, 1988; Crank, 2004) Law and Order (Niederhoffer, 1967) Safety and Uniformity (Crank, 2004)	Training, policy, and procedure (Kappeler, 1999) Culture (Crank, 2004) Unwritten rules (Quinn, 2005)	Appearance of police (e.g., uniform, gun, and badge) (Crank, 2004)
Structural	Jurisdiction (Jiao, 2001) Professionalism (Jiao, 2001) Law enforcement (Crank, 2004)	Skills, training, and hierarchical structure (Crank, 2004) Policy and procedure (Kappeler et al., 1998)	Rank (i.e. insignias and differences in uniforms) (Crank, 2004)
Human	Influence and power (Kappeler et al., 1998; Niederhoffer, 1967) Conflict resolution (Crank, 2004) Abuse of power (Quinn, 2005) Coercive force (Kappeler, 1999) Problem-solving (Jiao, 2001) Discretion (Brown, 1998) Shaped by politics/peers (Kappeler et al., 1999)	Communication (Quinn, 2005) Implicit and explicit knowledge (Nonaka & Nishiguchi, 2001)	Acceptable with in culture (Crank, 2004) Peer pressure (Jiao, 2001) Unwritten rules (Quinn, 2005) Responding in difficult situations (Crank, 2004)

APPENDIX B: INFORMED CONSENT FORM

UNIVERSITY OF PHOENIX

Informed Consent: Participants 18 years of age and older

Dear_____,

My name is Olivia N. Johnson and I am a student at the University of Phoenix working on a doctorate degree. I am conducting a research study titled The Blue Wall of Silence: Law Enforcement Officer's Perceptions of Training's Influence on Officer Suicide. The purpose of the research study is to explore the perceptions of White male law enforcement officers from Madison and St. Clair County, Illinois concerning the effects of mental health training on the incidence of suicide among law enforcement officers.

Your participation will involve providing insight based on personal perception about the role training has on preventing law enforcement suicide. Your participation in the study is voluntary. If you choose not to participate or to withdraw from the study at any time, you can do so without penalty or loss of benefit to yourself. The results of the research study may be published, but your identity will remain confidential and your name will not be disclosed to any outside party.

In the research, there are no foreseeable risks to you except the possibility of increased levels of stress due to the nature of the topic being discussed.

Although there may be no direct benefit to you, a possible benefit of your participation is a contribution to existing and future research about law enforcement suicide, in an attempt to save the lives of law enforcement personnel.

If you have any questions concerning the research study, please call me at ████████████ or by email at: ████████████████████

As a participant in this study, you should understand the following:

1. You may decline to participate or withdraw from participation at any time without consequences.
2. Your identity will be kept confidential.
3. Olivia Johnson the researcher, has thoroughly explained the parameters of the research study and all of your questions and concerns have been addressed.
4. If the interviews are recorded, you must grant permission for the researcher, Olivia Johnson, to digitally record the interview. You understand that the information from the recorded interviews may be transcribed. The researcher will structure a coding process to assure that anonymity of your name is protected.
5. Data will be stored in a secure and locked area. The data will be held for a period of 3 years and then destroyed.
6. The research results will be used for publication.

"By signing this form you acknowledge that you understand the nature of the study, the potential risks to you as a participant, and the means by which your identity will be kept confidential. Your signature on this form also indicates that you are 18 years old or older and that you give your permission to voluntarily serve as a participant in the study described."

Signature of the interviewee_____Date _____

Signature of the researcher_____Date _____

APPENDIX C: LETTER REQUESTING DEPARTMENT INVOLVEMENT

Hello, my name is Olivia Johnson. I am a doctoral student with the University of Phoenix, working on my dissertation, titled: The Blue Wall of Silence: Law Enforcement Officer's Perceptions of Training's Influence on Officer Suicide. The purpose of the study is to obtain perceptions and lived experiences of law enforcement officers about training's influence on the incidence of officer suicide. The participants of the study include sworn, full-time, White, male officers with a minimum of 5 years of law enforcement experience, working in Madison and St. Clair Counties, in Illinois law enforcement agencies. White, male law enforcement officers are appropriate because this population reflects the White, male population considered high-risk for suicide by the Center for Disease Control.

In the research, there are no foreseeable risks to participants except the possibility of increased levels of stress due to the nature of the topic discussed. Although there may be no direct benefit to participants, a possible benefit of participation is a contribution to existing and future research about law enforcement suicide, in an attempt to save the lives of law enforcement personnel. All participants must be 18 years of age or older and of sound mental health. Participants will be informed of the procedures of the research study. All eligible participants must complete and sign informed consent paperwork. The researcher will explain all procedures in advance to each participant, informing participants of possible risks or potential harm.

Participants will be informed of the voluntary nature of the study by receiving a copy of the informed consent paperwork and by the researcher verbally. Participants will be informed verbally and in the informed consent form that they can withdrawal at any time and for any reason without penalty. Participants can submit a withdrawal in writing, by email, in person, or by phone. Once a request to withdraw is received, the researcher will remove the participant from eligibility status, and a new eligible recipient will be chosen. If a participant declines further participation, an eligible replacement will not be chosen from the same department.

Permission must be received (i.e. verbal or written) from the department's Chief or equivalent, in order for your department to be considered for the study. Once departmental eligibility is declared, the researcher will ask for a maximum of two eligible officers to be chosen from any department. Eligible officers must meet the guidelines listed above. Please notify the researcher if your department is interested in participating in the study and to set up a date and time for interviews.

If you have any questions about your department or officer eligibility, please feel free to contact the researcher at ██████████████████████████████.

APPENDIX D: PERMISSION TO USE PREMISES, NAME, AND/OR SUBJECTS

UNIVERSITY OF PHOENIX

Permission to Use Premises, Name, and/or Subjects

(Facility, Organization, University, Institution, or Association)

Alton Illinois Police Department

Name of Facility, Organization, University, Institution, or Association

Check any that apply:

☑ I hereby authorize Olivia Johnson, student of University of Phoenix, to use the premises (facility identified below) to conduct a study entitled Breaking the Blue Wall of Silence: Officers' Perceptions of Training's Impact on Officer Suicide.

☑ I hereby authorize Olivia Johnson student of University of Phoenix, to recruit subjects for participation in a conduct a study entitled Breaking the Blue Wall of Silence: Officers' Perceptions of Training's Impact on Officer Suicide.

☑ I hereby authorize Olivia Johnson student of University of Phoenix, to use the name of the facility, organization, university, institution, or association identified above when publishing results from the study entitled Breaking Through the Blue Wall of Silence: Officers' Perceptions of Training's Impact on Officer Suicide.

Signature _David H Hayes_   Date _7/17/09_

Name _Maj. David H Hayes_   Title _Deputy Chief of Police_

Address of Facility

1700 East Broadway
Alton, Il. 62002

UNIVERSITY OF PHOENIX

Permission to Use Premises, Name, and/or Subjects

(Facility, Organization, University, Institution, or Association)

<u>Highland Illinois Police Department</u>

Name of Facility, Organization, University, Institution, or Association

Check any that apply:

[X] I hereby authorize Olivia Johnson, student of University of Phoenix, to use the premises (facility identified below) to conduct a study entitled Breaking the Blue Wall of Silence: Officers' Perceptions of Training's Impact on Officer Suicide.

[X] I hereby authorize Olivia Johnson student of University of Phoenix, to recruit subjects for participation in a conduct a study entitled Breaking the Blue Wall of Silence: Officers' Perceptions of Training's Impact on Officer Suicide.

[X] I hereby authorize Olivia Johnson student of University of Phoenix, to use the name of the facility, organization, university, institution, or association identified above when publishing results from the study entitled Breaking Through the Blue Wall of Silence: Officers' Perceptions of Training's Impact on Officer Suicide.

Signature _____ Date 07-12-09

Name Terry M. Bell Title Chief

Address of Facility

Highland P.D.
820 Mulberry
Highland, Il. 62249

UNIVERSITY OF PHOENIX

PERMISSION TO USE PREMISES, NAME, AND/OR SUBJECTS
(Facility, Organization, University, Institution, or Association)

<u>Collinsville Police Department</u>

Name of Facility, Organization, University, Institution, or Association

Check any that apply:

☑ I hereby authorize Olivia N. Johnson, student of University of Phoenix, to use the premises (facility identified below) to conduct a study entitled *Blue Wall of Silence: Perceptions of the Influence of Training on Law Enforcement Suicide.*

☑ I hereby authorize Olivia N. Johnson a student of University of Phoenix, to recruit subjects for participation in a study entitled *Blue Wall of Silence: Perceptions of the Influence of Training on Law Enforcement Suicide.*

☑ I hereby authorize Olivia N. Johnson, student of University of Phoenix, to use the name of the facility, organization, university, institution, or association identified above when publishing results from the study entitled *Blue Wall of Silence: Perceptions of the Influence of Training on Law Enforcement Suicide.*

Signature *Scott Williams*   Date 11/2/9

Scott Williams, Chief
200 West Clay
Collinsville, IL 62234
Name, Title, & Address of Facility

1